International Management English

Working Virtually

Jackie Black and Jon Dyson

DELTA Publishing
Quince Cottage
Hoe Lane
Peaslake
Surrey GU5 9SW
England

York Associates
Peasholme House
St Saviours Place
York YO1 7PJ
England

www.deltapublishing.co.uk

© DELTA Publishing and York Associates 2013

All rights reserved. No reproduction, copy or transmission of this publication may be made without written permission from the publishers or in accordance with the provisions of the Copyright, Designs and Patents Act 1988, or under the terms of any licence permitting copying issued by the Copyright Licensing Agency, Saffron House, 6–10 Kirby Street, London EC1N 8TS.

First published 2013

Edited by Catriona Watson-Brown
Designed by Caroline Johnston
Illustrations by Kathy Baxendale (pages 25, 44, 45, 61, 70, 80)
Cover design by Clare Webber
Cover photo © Shutterstock
Printed in Greece by Bakis

ISBN 978-1-905085-69-9

Acknowledgements

The authors would like to thank the following people for their help during the writing of the book:
Jackie Black: My family (Phil, Ben, Alex and Becky) for being so patient and feigning interest in my work at the right times; my friend Jayne for allowing me to base a case study on her; colleagues in Finland for taking the time to share their academic experience with me; Nick Brieger for pointing us in the right direction.
Jon Dyson: My family and friends for all their support.

The author and publishers are grateful to the following for permission to reproduce copyright material:

Figures
MIS Quarterly for a figure adapted from Daft, R.L., Lengel, R.H. and Trevino, L.K., Message Equivocality, Media Selection and Manager Performance: Implications for Information Systems, *MIS Quarterly* (11:3), 1987, pp. 355–366, Figure 1. Copyright © 1987, Regents of the University of Minnesota. Used with permission; RW3 Culture Wizard for Figures from *The Challenges of Working in Virtual Teams – Virtual Teams Survey Report* 2012, p.15, p.18, © 2012 RW3 LLC – All rights reserved.

Text
Academy of Management for an extract from *The determinants of trust in multicultural global virtual teams*, republished with permission of Academy of Management, from Academy of Management. Annual Meeting Proceedings, Audra I. Mockaitis, Elizabeth L. Rose, Peter Zettinig, 2009, 1, copyright © 2009, Academy of Management; permission conveyed through Copyright Clearance Center, Inc.; CBS News for an adapted extract from *4 Reasons Timezones and Language Matter to International Teams* by Wayne Turmel, 3 May 2010, from www.cbsnews.com/8301-505125_162-44240299/4-reasons-timezones-and-language-matter-to-international-teams; Linda DeLuca for an adapted extract from *How to be an artful collaborator*, http://azione-scopo.com/2010/09/10/how-to-be-an-artful-collaborator, © 2013 Linda DaLuca, Advisor, Coach, and Creator Azione-Scopo.com; John Folk-Williams for an adapted extract from *How diversity improves collaborative problem-solving*, from www.crosscollaborate.com/2010/05/diversity-improves-collaborative-problem-solving; John Ford for an adapted extracts from *Cross-cultural conflict resolution in teams*, from www.mediate.com/articles/ford5.cfm; Geert Hofstede B.V. for an adapted extract from Geert Hofstede, Gert Jan Hofstede, Michael Minkov, *Cultures and Organizations, Software of the Mind*, Third Revised Edition, McGraw Hill 2010, ISBN 0-07-166418-1. © Geert Hofstede B.V. quoted with permission; Interaction Associates for an adapted extract from *Managing Online Meetings: Keeping People Engaged – Survey Results and Tactics for Success*, Interaction Associates White Paper, pp. 9–10; Laurie McCabe for an extract from *What's a collaboration suite and why should you care?*, 30 June 2010, from www.smallbusinesscomputing.com/biztools/article.php/3890601/Whats-a-Collaboration-Suite--Why-Should-You-Care.htm; Plain English Campaign for *How to write in plain English*, from www.plainenglish.co.uk.

In some instances we have been unable to trace the owners of copyright material and we would appreciate any information that would enable us to do so.

Photo on page 84 courtesy of Geert Hofstede.
Photo on page 10 (bottom) courtesy of Vaula Aunola.
Cartoon on page 24 © Lee Lambert, courtesy of Lambert Consulting Group, Inc.
Cartoon on page 35 courtesy of DILBERT © 2013 Scott Adams. Used by permission of UNIVERSAL UCLICK. All rights reserved.
Photo on page 38 courtesy of Jon Dyson.
iStock: pages 8, 33 (left), 40, 50, 60 (all), 68 (both), 80
Shutterstock: pages 10 (top), 19, 28, 29, 33 (right), 35 (top), 45, 51, 52, 54 (both), 64, 65, 71, 78
Cartoonstock: pages 13, 21, 30, 43, 61
Pixmac.com: page 75

Contents

Introduction 4
Learning diary 5
Needs analysis 6

1 Understanding virtual communication
A Discussion and listening 8
B Communication skills: Adapting your communication style 10
C Professional skills: Key competences for working virtually 12
D Intercultural competence: How culture affects virtual communication 14
Case study: Why are we underperforming? 15
E Language reference 16
F Virtual working tips and personal action plan 17

2 Preparing for successful communication
A Discussion and listening 18
B Communication skills: Planning effective virtual meetings 20
C Professional skills: Keeping people focused 22
D Intercultural competence: Thinking beyond the department 24
Case study: An issue with sharing information 25
E Language reference 26
F Virtual working tips and personal action plan 27

3 Working in virtual groups
A Discussion and listening 28
B Communication skills: Language skills for conference calls 30
C Professional skills: Success factors in virtual meetings 32
D Intercultural competence: Cross-cultural presentation skills 34
Case study: Different international presentation styles 35
E Language reference 36
F Virtual working tips and personal action plan 37

4 Working with technology
A Discussion and listening 38
B Communication skills: The range of communication channels 40
C Professional skills: Choosing technology for collaboration and engagement 42
D Intercultural competence: Cultural diversity and technology use 44
Case study: The virtual inbox 45
E Language reference 46
F Virtual working tips and personal action plan 47

5 Effective writing
A Discussion and listening 48
B Communication skills: Being clear and concise 50
C Professional skills: Choosing the right content and technical level 52
D Intercultural competence: Cultural differences in writing 54
Case study: The right message? 55
E Language reference 56
F Virtual working tips and personal action plan 57

6 Building relationships
A Discussion and listening 58
B Communication skills: Effective virtual interpersonal skills 60
C Professional skills: Creating and sustaining trust 62
D Intercultural competence: Managing conflict caused by cultural differences 64
Case study: The international quality standards team 65
E Language reference 66
F Virtual working tips and personal action plan 67

7 Managing diversity
A Discussion and listening 68
B Communication skills: Adapting communication styles 70
C Professional skills: Using diversity for effective collaboration 72
D Intercultural competence: Awareness of cultural diversity 74
Case study: Crossed wires 75
E Language reference 76
F Virtual working tips and personal action plan 77

8 Teams and leadership
A Discussion and listening 78
B Communication skills: Skills for motivating and involving 80
C Professional skills: Team-building in a virtual environment 82
D Intercultural competence: How culture affects leaders and teams 84
Case study: EasyFix 85
E Language reference 86
F Virtual working tips and personal action plan 87

Activity file 88
Audio script 95
Answer key 106
Word list 114

Introduction

At York Associates, we always aim to develop the skills which help professionals to do their jobs better. In recent years, we have worked hard to enrich our Business English and professional communication training with intercultural content. More recently, we have included a focus on important interpersonal and management skills for listening, building relationships and trust, influencing, etc.

Our approach is built on the premise that good communication is vital to achieving results at work. Effective international communicators need a blend of language, professional communication, intercultural and management skills to be successful.

Welcome to *International Management English*, a new series published jointly by York Associates and Delta Publishing. The four titles in this series are:
- *Leading People*
- *Managing Projects*
- *Working Virtually*
- *Managing Change*

Each book includes either one or two audio CDs.

Professional language training with a management focus

Each book consists of eight units of study, containing four sections per unit:
- ***Section A: Discussion and listening***
  Engaging and relevant content in areas of international management and teamwork
- ***Section B: Communication skills***
  Opportunities for the practice of key skills in areas such as conflict management, team-building and giving/receiving feedback, as well as more familiar topics such as presentations, meetings, negotiations and writing e-mails
- ***Section C: Professional skills***
  Authentic texts from leading management writers and thinkers, designed to encourage reflection and debate among readers
- ***Section D: Intercultural competence and Case study***
  A focus on raising intercultural awareness, followed by an illustrative case study drawn from the authors' experience of the international business world

In addition, each unit offers:
- a strong emphasis on vocabulary learning, with glossaries of key terms at the end of each unit
- practical tips on how to improve performance at work
- the opportunity to use a learning diary, which encourages the setting of realistic goals to implement the learning points from each unit.

At the end of the book, the Word list provides a useful list of key words, referenced to the first occurrence of each word.

Having worked through the book, you will have developed not only your business language skills but also your ability to communicate and manage real challenges in your international working environment.

To the teacher

The four titles in this series represent a new development in ELT. They broaden the scope of teaching to include highly relevant management topics and skills. The materials are not only engaging for teachers, allowing them to introduce and develop new management communication skills in an ELT classroom; students are also motivated as they learn how to manage real professional communication challenges which they face at work on a daily basis.

Each title is designed primarily for work with both small and larger groups, but can also be used in one-to-one situations and has many features which will support self-study.

Across the eight units of each title, there is a strong focus on developing fluency and skills to communicate effectively in real work situations. There are opportunities to practise listening, reading and writing skills. The intercultural case studies in Section D are drawn from real-life examples and provide engaging discussion and problem-solving material for the ELT classroom.

There is online support for trainers (www.delta publishing.co.uk/resources) in the form of notes for each unit, which provide background information on the management topics and skills presented.

A final word

To both learner and teacher, we would like to express the hope that you find the materials stimulating, and that they help people to communicate more effectively at work.

Learning diary

Accelerate your learning by using this Learning diary. Make eight photocopies of this page, one for each unit. Note down important new words and expressions from the unit as you study. Make notes to help you remember any good advice you get on how to communicate and be effective across cultures. Then decide on some actions you can take to help to consolidate the things you have learned.

Unit number: _____

1 Language
Important (new) words and expressions for me from this unit are:

2 Professional communication skills
Important (new) expressions and communication tips for me from this unit are:

3 Intercultural competence
Important information/tips to be effective across cultures for me from this unit are:

4 Actions
To help me to consolidate all the learning points above, I need to:

Needs analysis

Introduction
You can use this Needs analysis to help you think about how to make the most of this course and to maximise your learning.

Managing your communication network
Think about who you communicate with in English. Draw a diagram to represent your network of communications, showing the important individuals or groups of people you communicate with. Follow the example and note down the channel of communication you use, e.g. face-to-face, phone, video conference, e-mail, etc.

How effectively do you use your network? Are you connecting with the right people in the best way at the most appropriate time? Are you spending enough time communicating with each individual or group?
Brainstorm some ideas for ways in which you could use your network more effectively.

I should spend more time planning my longer e-mails rather than writing them quickly and sending without considering the message. That way, I would get a more positive response from some colleagues.

Your communication needs
What do you have to do in English, and how challenging is it? Build your own communication profile by completing the following tables for virtual communication skills, professional communication skills and interpersonal skills. Tick (✓) the tasks you most commonly do. Then note down how challenging you find it, using a scale of 1 to 5 (1 = very easy, 2 = easy, 3 = occasional problems, 4 = challenging, 5 = very difficult). If you score 3 or more for a task, write down a reason why it is challenging.

Virtual communication skills

skill	✓	scale of challenge
Using the best channel of communication		
Dealing with the technology you use		
Writing correctly and coherently		
Getting your message across in online meetings		
Getting information to complete tasks		
Connecting with people in different parts of the world		
Working in teams where you rarely meeting other members face to face		
Other		

Professional communication skills

skill	✓	scale of challenge
Presenting		
Meeting		
Negotiating		
Writing (reports, e-mails, etc.)		
Socialising		
Decision-making		
Problem-solving		
Other		

Interpersonal skills

skill	✓	scale of challenge
Building and maintaining relationships		
Networking		
Building and maintaining trust		
Influencing people		
Listening actively		
Managing conflict		
Other		

Your language and communication challenges You work virtually in an international context and you use a foreign language to do so. What are the biggest language and communication challenges that you face?
1 ....
2 ....
3 ....

Your intercultural challenges What are the biggest intercultural challenges that you face?
1 ....
2 ....
3 ....

Your current learning objectives What would most help you to improve your ability to communicate effectively in an international virtual context?
1 ....
2 ....
3 ....

Your future learning targets As part of your learning plan, what targets can you fix for yourself? Start a learning diary (see page 5) and set yourself targets for future learning using this frame:
In one month's time, I aim to be able to ....
In three months' time, I aim to be able to ....
In six months' time, I aim to be able to ....
In one year's time, I aim to be able to ....

Needs analysis

1 Understanding virtual communication

AIMS
A To define virtual communication
B To adapt your communication style
C To develop key competences for working virtually
D To learn how culture affects virtual communication

A Discussion and listening

Think about it 1 Here is one definition of virtual communication.
'All interactions and relationships that occur not in a physical space but on the Internet through technological media'
What does *virtual communication* mean to you? How important is it for your organisation? Exchange ideas with a partner.

2 How many different types of virtual communication can you think of?
Work with a partner to add to this list.
Skype, SMS, Twitter, blogging, …

3 a How much of your time (both inside and outside work) do you spend communicating virtually?

  b Of the types of communication you listed in Exercise 2, which do you use?

Listen to this 4 a   1–3 Listen to three people talking about the different ways they communicate virtually. As you listen, complete the first three columns of this table.

name	job	technology used	opinion/attitude
Bettina		e-mail, instant messaging, …	
	team leader		• conference calls useful …
Chantou			

  b   1–3 Listen again and complete the fourth column of the table.

5 Exchange ideas with a partner on your own experiences of using virtual communication.

Focus on language

6 a Match the sentence beginnings (1–7) with the endings (a–g) to form examples of tasks mentioned in Exercise 4.

1 Report to
2 Attend
3 Invest time
4 Send
5 Share screens
6 Solve problems
7 Exchange ideas

a to edit documents together.
b weekly calls.
c in real time with IM*.
d and opinions with global colleagues.
e files as attachments.
f in building virtual relationships.
g senior managers by phone.

* instant messaging

b Which form of communication is each task most commonly used with?

7 Complete each of these sentences using the correct form of a suitable phrase from Exercise 6a.

a .... can be a very efficient way to ask colleagues to comment on your documents.
b It is vital that all stakeholders .... our .... in order to keep up to date.
c Looking back on the virtual project, I realise it was essential to .... in getting to know the team better.
d The most secure way to transfer large .... is to .... them as encrypted ....
e Using messaging apps is the most successful way of .... in .... time.
f As there is never time to meet face to face, I like the fact that I can .... with our global partners by setting up a conference call at a moment's notice.
g His busy workload means he has to .... his .... by phone.

Let's talk

8 a Think about your daily work and the tasks you need to do. Discuss with a partner which of these you feel you are good at. You can use examples from the previous exercises or add other kinds of tasks.

b Now think about the work you do (or will do) virtually. Which skills do you think you need to improve in order to become an effective virtual communicator?

1 Understanding virtual communication

B Communication skills: Adapting your communication style

Think about it 1 Look at the range of communication styles below. Where do you think you are on the scale? Discuss this in your group and compare your results.
Example: *I am more task oriented, probably because I work in production and have to deal with urgent problems on a regular basis. So I don't want to waste too much time with chatting.*

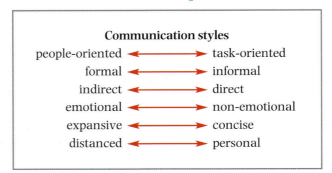

2 How far can you adapt your communication style to different people and situations? Which styles work well when communicating virtually? Why?

Listen to this 3 🎧 4 Listen to Jorma, a university teacher from Finland. How does he adapt his communication style to the virtual environment in his classes?

4 🎧 4 Listen again and decide whether each of these statements is true (T) or false (F).
a Jorma finds using technology demanding. F
b He pays attention to the volume of his voice.
c Speaking fast keeps everyone on board.
d Finns need time to think before they answer a question.
e Teachers need to check understanding more frequently if they are teaching virtually.

10 1 Understanding virtual communication

5 🎧 **5** Listen to the second part of the interview with Jorma and answer these questions.
   a Which major challenges does he talk about?
   b Which actions does he recommend to deal with these challenges?

6 What do you think are the advantages and disadvantages of distance learning?

Focus on language 7 a In the interview, Jorma uses a number of phrases to manage his communication more effectively. Look at these examples, then match each of the expressions in the box below with the correct headings (a–f).
   a **Reformulate**
      In other words, …
   b **Clarify**
      So, what you are saying is …
   c **Motivate**
      That's a good idea, Paolo.
   d **Show understanding**
      I appreciate your point.
   e **Indicate agreement**
      I absolutely agree with what Gemma said.
   f **Request more detail**
      Laura, can you expand on that second point, please?

> What do you mean exactly by … ?
> Could you say a little more about … ?
> Yes, I see what you mean.
> You've made a valuable point.
> Exactly!
> If I understand you correctly, you want to …

   b Think of more phrases which you could use under these headings.

Let's talk 8 a Work in groups of three. Appoint a speaker (A), a responder (B) and an observer (C). Using the topic list below or a topic of your choice, Student A speaks to Student B. Student B responds and summarises to Student A. Student C gives feedback on clear communication and successful outcome.

After about two or three minutes, Student C should stop the conversation and give feedback to Students A and B on their communication.

Topic list
- Teleconferences are largely a waste of time.
- E-mailing is the best way to communicate clearly.
- Twitter encourages you to express ideas more concisely.
- Blogging is a good way to build team spirit.

   b Now change roles and choose a different topic, making sure that everyone has the chance to be an active listener and to use the new language and expressions.

C Professional skills: Key competences for working virtually

Think about it 1 What do you think are the most important competences for working virtually? Brainstorm with your colleagues. Why are these competences so important?

Read this 2 The four blogs below are taken from a discussion forum on best practice in virtual communication. The four bloggers are people from different parts of the world with wide experience in this area. Answer these questions in your own words using their comments and opinions.
   a According to bloggers A and C, what are the main factors for successful virtual teamwork?
   b What do you understand by the term *buy-in* (blogger D)?
   c Which blogger:
      1 comments on the effect that unreliability can have?
      2 observes the effect of different ways of communicating?
      3 has a problem with local management demands on a team member?

A

I always try to act towards my colleagues in the way that I would like my team members to act towards each other. One person I always remember is an Indian colleague. He was a team leader who was very good at making you feel valued and important. He always made a point of thanking everyone for their contributions and for all their effort. The team had some very diverse personalities, but his approach, and the way he inspired us, made us all feel part of something, and that improved our performance, without a doubt ...

B

This colleague had a great mind and was a brilliant contributor when he wanted to be. But he was sometimes hard to get hold of; for example, he wouldn't always answer his phone, and he didn't reply to e-mails very promptly. Sometimes this meant that I missed deadlines, which is very annoying when it isn't your fault! On the whole, his contributions were greater than his deficiencies, but he simply wasn't reliable at times.

C

It's interesting to see the way in which different personalities approach communication. I have some colleagues who like to be very direct. They sometimes sound a little impolite! There are others who much prefer to have a chat about non-work subjects before we begin the business part of the call. Our team leader needs to act as a kind of 'policeman' during conference calls, because some people can get pretty emotional. Personally, I use e-mails for fact-based issues, and if I think emotion will be involved, I pick up the phone and speak to my colleague individually.

D

To be honest, it's very difficult to find the balance between keeping in contact with them and not being intrusive in their daily work. But sometimes, getting 'buy-in' from a team member halfway across the world is a major problem, especially when their primary loyalty has to be to the local line manager. Right now, I have a woman from Indonesia who is a very hard-working and intelligent team member. But she has a line manager in her country who seems to make demands on her time when she needs to be producing documents for my team. This is the problem when other team members worldwide depend on her work.

3 Use the blogs to answer these questions.
  a How did the Indian colleague's qualities help his team?
  b Why is it important to gain 'buy-in' from team members?

4 Choose one of the blog entries and write a short reply/contribution, giving some brief information about your own circumstances, as well as something about your experience of virtual communication and team work. You could also ask some questions to encourage others to join the discussion thread!

Focus on language

5 The bloggers raise important issues about the range of skills, qualities and attitudes required when working in a virtual environment. Match the words and phrases in the box with their definitions (a–i) below.

> availability   autonomy   ~~engagement~~   networking skills   predictability
> reliability   self-awareness   team spirit   trust

  a Demonstrating full and undivided attention to a task or event   *engagement*
  b The capacity to work alone without guidance from managers if necessary
  c Showing consistent behaviour or attitudes
  d Being dependable and delivering what you promise
  e An attitude of goodwill and belief in the capabilities of others
  f Knowing and acknowledging your strengths and weaknesses in specific areas
  g Showing the skills and attitude to work with others towards a common goal
  h Being there when people need to contact you
  i Having the interpersonal skills to communicate effectively in a socialising situation

6 Complete each of these sentences with the appropriate form of a word or phrase from Exercise 7.
  a He doesn't seem to be very *engaged* in our teleconferences. He's always tapping away on his phone while we're speaking.
  b She's very .... because she always delivers quality on time.
  c There's a real feeling of .... amongst us, even though we never see each other.
  d She lacks experience, but has a lot of energy. I'm sure if we .... in her abilities, she'll prove her value.
  e I think .... is important – everyone should be able to work alone and use their judgement.
  f Everyone knows I'm always .... between 10:00 and 16:00 CET.
  g She's incredibly good at .... – she knows exactly how to get to know complete strangers in five minutes!
  h He's totally transparent, even on the phone. He's .... because you know he'll be critical, but his comments are fair!
  i I like to think I'm .... -............... . I know I interrupt too much in conference calls, but I'm trying to stop myself from doing it.

Let's talk

7 Discuss these questions in small groups.
  a To what extent do you think differences in personality are an advantage or a disadvantage for virtual teamworking?
  b How important is reliability when working virtually?
  c How can you develop real trust among colleagues who work virtually?

'You have smartphone dependency, also known as compulsive communication syndrome.'

1 Understanding virtual communication

D Intercultural competence: How culture affects virtual communication

1 a What are good characteristics for communicating well with international colleagues? Are you good at it? Why? / Why not?

b Decide if the characteristics of communication in this box are positive or negative.

> simple/complex   expansive/brief   humorous/serious
> structured/unstructured   general/detailed   personal/impersonal

c Compare your opinions with a partner. Do you agree?

d Why might people from other parts of the world select different characteristics from your choices? Can you think of some examples?

2 🎧 6–7 Listen to two telephone conversations between colleagues. For each speaker, identify their communication styles from the list below.

Conversation 1: Erik and Mercedes
Conversation 2: Haruka and Monica

- structured/unstructured
- expansive/brief
- turn-taking/interrupting
- task-focused/people-focused

3 🎧 6–7 Listen to the conversations again and decide whether each of these statements is true (T) or false (F).
a Erik and Mercedes speak at different speeds.
b Mercedes pauses more than Erik.
c Mercedes thinks Erik is not there at the end of the conversation.
d Monica wants to chat informally at the start.
e Haruka doesn't want to talk about details.
f Haruka has problems understanding Monica.

4 How do you think the four speakers feel after the calls? With your partner, discuss your own impressions of the calls. Is the result of each call likely to be positive or not?

5 a A lot of virtual communication is in written form. The two e-mails below send the same message but in different ways. Read them both and answer these questions.
   a What is the purpose of the message?
   b How is the focus of the message different in the two e-mails?
   c How is the *written style* different in the two e-mails?

b Discuss your answers with a partner. Which e-mail do you prefer? Why?

E-mail A

Hi Jiri,
How was your weekend? Did you manage to get away? Unfortunately, I was tied up with the problems in the plant on Saturday, but we relaxed on Sunday.
Anyway, what's the news on Bratislava? Any luck with Petr? He's certainly on the ball, but not great when it comes to letting us know what's happening. Anyway, I'm sure you have it under control, but do me a favour – give me a status update when you can because Regina is very interested in the outcome. Much appreciated. We'll catch up by phone later.
Cheers,
Jon

E-mail B

Jiri,
Did you manage to solve the situation with the power cut-out in Bratislava? Did you spek to Petr and get some kind of asurance on stability?Let me know asap, cos Regina wants meto update her NOW.
Jon

6 The comments below illustrate certain attitudes when communicating virtually. Discuss these questions in groups.
   a Do any of the comments reflect how you feel?
   b Have you ever had to deal with people who typically say these things?
   c Have opinions like this ever created any problems in your working relationships?

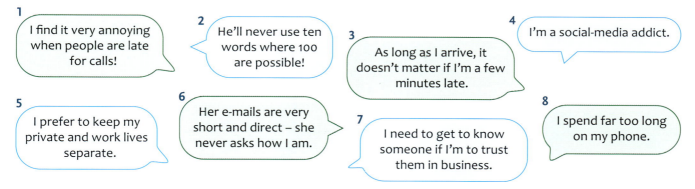

1 I find it very annoying when people are late for calls!
2 He'll never use ten words where 100 are possible!
3 As long as I arrive, it doesn't matter if I'm a few minutes late.
4 I'm a social-media addict.
5 I prefer to keep my private and work lives separate.
6 Her e-mails are very short and direct – she never asks how I am.
7 I need to get to know someone if I'm to trust them in business.
8 I spend far too long on my phone.

Case study: Why are we underperforming?

Background Frank Habner (an Austrian) works for Ebro, a French company selling a range of household goods worldwide on the Internet. It has operations in eight markets and has a market share of around 14% for these kinds of product.

Frank is currently leading a project team responsible for technical improvements to the company's web platform. The team consists of nine people distributed across Europe, Latin America and Asia, and its members are a mixture of business process developers and technical specialists.

Situation The project was set up very quickly because improvements in competitors' website displays required quick action to avoid falling behind the rest of the market. There was no time for a face-to-face kick-off meeting, and the team's organisation evolved in an unplanned way over the first few weeks. This project is not the primary responsibility of any team member, accounting for about 20% of their weekly working hours on average.

One of Frank's team, Zoe Wei from Singapore, sent him this e-mail last night.

> To: Frank Habner
> From: Zoe Wei
>
> Hello Frank,
> Just to let you know Javier has missed the deadline again. He knows I need information, but he's never at his desk when I call him and he doesn't answer his e–mails. Will you have a word?
> One more thing. I think the last conference call was a disaster. Hans is very annoying when he interrupts all the time and he was really rude to Yolanda. She was furious! I know it isn't easy for you, running the meeting, taking the minutes and trying to contribute too, but I think some members of the team will soon feel alienated, which will affect performance and results.
> Can we discuss this at the start of the next conference call?
> Thanks.
> Zoe

Task In groups, discuss these questions.
   a What are the factors affecting the team's performance?
   b What could be the negative consequence of each factor?
   c If you were Frank, what would you do to categorise and prioritise action?
   d Why is cultural awareness important when addressing issues like these?

One person in each group should take notes on the discussion and give a short summary of the group's views.

1 Understanding virtual communication

E Language reference

Read through the key words and phrases below from this unit. Add any other useful words and expressions which you feel are important for you to learn. Make sure you find the time to review these words and phrases regularly and to use them at work.

Key factors for successful virtual communication

to create team spirit	clarity
to foster bonds	trust
flexibility	loyalty
transparency	

Communication styles

formal/informal	big-picture/detailed
direct/indirect	structured/linear
emotional/non-emotional	unstructured/organic
expansive/brief	time-limited/time-fluid
people-oriented/task-oriented	

Virtual competences

achieve 'buy in' (commitment and agreement)
engage the team/audience
show empathy
be on the same wavelength (as someone)
collaborate with (other team members)
deliver results
accept a challenge
enhance performance/results
gain consensus
influence someone / a decision
share knowledge/expertise
clarify
motivate
reformulate (a question / a statement)
summarise

Culture

work with diverse personalities
be aware of cultural differences
address cultural misunderstanding

Virtual activities and tasks

design and present documents	monitor progress
manage communication technology	exchange ideas
plan and set up conference calls	find solutions
facilitate a meeting	build relationships
take minutes	keep to deadlines
establish ground rules	deal with problems
network with colleagues	report to managers
write and respond to e-mails	edit documents

Writing task Choose one of these e-mail writing activities. Integrate at least five of the virtual-communication words above into the e-mail of your choice.

1 Your manager has asked you to facilitate an international kick-off video conference. Write a short e-mail to all the participants outlining some ground rules you want to establish to ensure the meeting runs smoothly.
2 Your manager could not attend your team's most recent conference call. She received a copy of the minutes, but would like your views on how successful the meeting was. Send a short e-mail giving your opinion.

F Virtual working tips and personal action plan

1 Take a few minutes to reflect on these tips for virtual communication which arise from this unit. How far do you agree with each one? Which do you think is the most important, and which ideas are the most useful?

TIP 1
Virtual communication is very different from face-to-face interaction, so you need to think carefully about the impact of the way you communicate on other people and be prepared, if required, to adapt your style. For example, if your preferred style is silent listening, you need to become more verbal in your responses, or the person on the other end of the line will not be clear if you are following or not. Try to analyse your own communication style in more detail and think about situations where this style had positive or negative outcomes.
Ideas to help you think about your style:
- Record yourself participating in a conference call or phone conversation. Listen to it and evaluate your own contribution and the effect it has on other people. What aspects could you change? What are your strengths?
- Try acting and behaving in a different way to how you would normally behave in your next virtual conversation. If you speak a lot, speak less and ask more questions. If you never practise small talk with the other person, try doing it. Change the normal!

TIP 2
It is extremely important to establish positive and meaningful relationships at a very early stage of your virtual communication (e.g. in a project team). It is easy to focus too heavily on tasks and their completion, when what you need to remember is that there is another person on the other end of the line.
Ideas to help build virtual relationships:
- Ask team or group members to share something of their backgrounds and life outside the virtual environment so that everybody can build a mental picture of each other.
- Encourage (or even insist on) small talk at the beginning of each conference call so that participants recognise the importance of relationship-building.

TIP 3
Much virtual communication is international, across time zones, continents and cultures. It is important to be aware of diversity and local context. This includes diversity of opinion, which you should encourage. Value different views, because that will create a positive attitude to differences and may even stimulate innovation.
Ideas to encourage diversity:
- State at the beginning of conference calls that different opinions are welcome.
- Make sure you manage this diversity by including everyone and valuing contributions equally.

	what I learned and want to apply to my job	when/how I will apply this in my job	how I will check if I have applied it
1			
2			
3			

Preparing for successful communication

AIMS
A To look at the four Ps of successful communication
B To plan effective virtual meetings
C To learn how to keep people focused
D To think beyond the department

A Discussion and listening

Think about it 1 How do you prepare for virtual communication? Look at this checklist. How far do you agree with it? Discuss your answers with a partner. Can you add anything to the list?

> **Preparation checklist**
> - Decide which channel of communication best fits the task.
> - Consider the purpose of your communication carefully.
> - Check the time zones of people you are going to communicate with.
> - Make sure any equipment you need is working properly.
> - For a teleconference, think about the different people attending and their needs (e.g. language).
> - Prepare any visual aids / notes to assist you.
> - Decide which roles you want people to take (e.g. leading a teleconference).

2 How much time do you spend preparing for a virtual meeting or teleconference? Is it enough?

Listen to this 3 🎧 8 Listen to what Michael Laing, a communication expert, says about the 'four Ps' of business communication. As you listen, make a note of the four different key words he mentions.
   a P...............   b P...............   c P...............   d P...............

4 🎧 8 Listen again and tick which of these points Michael makes.
   a It is essential to prepare in some way or another. ☐
   b If you state clearly why you are doing something, there will be no need for clarification later. ☐
   c Go through the process step by step so that everyone knows how you want them to interact. ☐
   d Think carefully about the people you are about to communicate with. ☐
   e The best results are achieved by adopting a flexible approach. ☐
   f You need to practise virtual communication to get the balance right. ☐

5 Which of the four Ps do you think is the most important? Which one do you spend most time thinking about?

Focus on language

6 Complete these phrases with verbs from Track 8.
a M.aximise... the outcomes.
b D............ o............ the timing.
c D............ u............ the agenda.
d C............ relevant information.
e M............ your expectations clear.
f C............ understanding.
g G............ through the process.
h A............ a flexible approach.
i A............ better results
j G............ the balance right

7 Complete each of these sentences using a phrase from Exercise 6.
a If you don't ...., nobody knows how long the meeting is likely to last.
b In my opinion, her ideas are too fixed. She needs to .... a more ....
c The meeting was a complete disaster because no one had .... the .... beforehand, so we didn't know what we were supposed to discuss.
d This year has been very disappointing for us. If we had worked harder, we would have ....
e He spent a long time preparing the agenda to make sure he was able to .... in the meeting and not waste valuable time.

8 Work in pairs or small groups using the 'four Ps' model to produce a list of best practices for planning and preparation.
Preparation: *decide on items for agenda, ...*
Purpose:
Process:
People:

Let's talk

9 Look at the list of communication channels below. Choose one of them and discuss with a partner how you could improve communication in your organisation through that channel, using the four Ps.

Example: *E-mail: we could reduce the number of irrelevant e-mails by thinking more carefully about who is copied in.*

- e-mail
- blog
- instant messaging
- phone
- video/teleconference

2 Preparing for successful communication

B Communication skills: Planning effective virtual meetings

Think about it 1 Think of someone you know who manages meetings well. How do they do this? Which skills are necessary? What do you need to think about when preparing to manage a virtual meeting?

Listen to this 2 🎧 9 Listen to the first part of a presentation by a trainer to a group of young managers. What is the purpose of this presentation? To what extent do you agree with the trainer?

3 Answer these questions about the presentation.
   a What does the trainer tell the managers about who to invite?
   b How does the trainer advise the managers to put their audience at ease before the meeting?
   c What should the managers do to ensure the best outcome?

4 🎧 10 Listen to the second part of the presentation. What does the trainer say about these subjects?
   a time zones
   b rules
   c technology

5 The trainer recommends spending time at the beginning of the meeting encouraging small talk. What do you think?

Focus on language 6 🎧 10 Listen to the second part of the presentation again and find words or phrases which mean the same as these ones.
   a send round documents   *circulate documents*
   b consider
   c guidelines
   d join a meeting
   e solve (a problem)

7 a Here are some of the key tasks to consider when planning a virtual meeting or presentation. Match each of the expressions below (1–12) with the correct task (a–f).

   a Establish rules
   b Decide on timing
   c Build rapport
   d Outline purpose / desired outcome
   e Request action
   f Keep participants focused

   1 This meeting will last 45 minutes.
   2 I think we should aim to finish by lunchtime.
   3 The aim of today's meeting is to discuss the latest budget proposals.
   4 We must report our findings to the Board by the end of the week.
   5 Could you switch your mobile phones off and use the mute button when not speaking?
   6 I really need to hear everyone's position on this issue.
   7 John, would you be able to look into the cost of repairs, please?
   8 Thank you all for logging in on time. How is everyone?
   9 Can everyone say a few words about what they've been doing?
   10 I know you're all busy, but I'd appreciate your input.
   11 No one should be checking their e-mails during this meeting.
   12 Ulrike, I need you and Xian to contact our suppliers immediately.

b Read the expressions on page 20 again and decide if each one is direct or indirect in style.

Example: 1 direct, 2 indirect, 3 …

Let's talk **8** Imagine you have been sent this feedback on the last meeting you managed. Discuss with a partner what you would do to avoid this happening again. Use this feedback to write a checklist to help you prepare for your next meeting.

Example: Plan the agenda more carefully. Try to estimate the timing for each item.

Subject: Weekly team meeting

Overall evaluation

- *Timing*: Much too long. We could have covered most of the points on the agenda in half the time.
- *Distribution of information pre-meeting*: Insufficient: the key data was not available before the meeting.
- *Relevance*: Not really relevant to me.
- *Facilitation*: Purpose not very clear. Action plan poorly defined.

9 Work with a partner.

Student A: You are the facilitator from the meeting in Exercise 8. Find out exactly what the issues are and decide if you agree or disagree with your team member's feedback.

Student B: You are a team member offering feedback on the meeting. Try to sound constructive and make suggestions on how to improve the process.

2 Preparing for successful communication

C Professional skills: Keeping people focused

Think about it 1 How often do you go to a meeting where people are checking their e-mails or sending texts instead of participating fully in the meeting? Why do you think this happens?

Read this 2 This extract is based on a survey of 200 business professionals carried out by Interaction Associates in 2009. Read the extract, then answer the questions on page 23.

More so than with in-person meetings, the challenges for virtual collaboration can be daunting at many companies. The most significant issues ('always or often a challenge') include:

Getting everyone focused and participating:	74%
People multi-tasking and not paying attention:	74%
Creating an exciting visual experience:	66%
Building relationships with others:	54%
Keeping the meeting on track:	33%

No doubt these are the same challenges that you deal with, so let's explore tips and best practices that address them.

TIP 1
Keep people focused with regular interaction

At critical points in the meeting, when team agreement is being reached or when input is required, go around the virtual room and call everyone by name, asking if they agree or have an idea to share.

Participants in the virtual meeting have no visual cues which tell them when it is their turn to speak. Meeting leaders may say: 'What do you all think?' as a way of getting input. That technique is not sufficient to generate input and get agreement.

Instead, actually call each member by name. If you have just presented the context for the meeting and want to make sure everyone understands it before you move to the first topic, ask: 'Martha, does that make sense to you?' and Martha would reply: 'Yes.' 'Alice, did you get all that?' and Alice would reply: 'Check.' And so on, until everyone in the group has had a turn to respond.

This technique may seem time-consuming, but participants report a significant increase in feelings of inclusion and control when the meeting leader takes the time to check with each person by name. It also reduces the incidence of virtual participants multi-tasking and dozing off if they know they may be called on to give input at any time.

Mix up this verbal technique with the use of the 'raise hands' or 'checkmark' features on your online meeting platform. Go for variety, and participation will rise.

TIP 2
Keep people focused with colour commentary

When there is some kind of activity going on at the meeting leader's location, it is helpful to describe to remote listeners what is happening. For instance, 'We're waiting a moment while Mimi gets out the notes' or 'Everyone in (Phoenix) appears to agree with the points that are being made. Let's check with (Salt Lake)'. These verbal commentaries make the meeting more 'real' to virtual participants and increase feelings of inclusion and openness. It is also helpful to review progress and summarise discussions as you go. These periodic reviews and summaries help keep people focused on the task in hand.

TIP 3
Keep people focused with compelling visuals

Striking, interactive or even humorous visuals can help people stay tuned in during the meeting. As you present material, illustrate it with visuals rather than text. Brainstormed 'lists' or meeting notes can be created on the spot in web meetings, so that all participants have access to the same group decisions. If you are using PowerPoint, be sure to replace the bullet points with plenty of surprising visuals. These presentations can be used to guide people through a detailed presentation without losing track of the main ideas.

Tip 1

a When is it best to go round the virtual room and call everyone by name?
b Why is it more difficult for participants to know when it is their turn to speak?
c Why is it not sufficient to ask 'What do you all think?'?
d How do participants feel when the meeting leader checks with them all by name?
e What other consequence does this activity have?

Tip 2

f How can you increase participant engagement?
g What is meant by *colour commentary*?

Tip 3

h In what other ways can you keep people focused during the meeting?
i What is the main purpose of using visuals in a meeting?

3 Discuss these questions with a partner.

a Why can it be difficult to keep people focused during a teleconference?
b In your organisation, do you have rules for meetings, for example about the use of mobile devices?
c How do you keep people focused in your meetings?

Focus on language

4 The survey gives tips on how to improve virtual collaboration through regular interaction. Use verbs in the box on the left to complete the gapped sentences so that they mean the same as the sentences on the right.

give
hear
lead
look at
make
present

a Martha, does that .... sense? — Martha, is that clear?
b David, would you .... us a summary, please? — David, can you sum up?
c I'd like Angela to .... this point. — Angela, take us through this point, please.
d Could you .... the next slide, Pavel? — Can you go through the next slide, Pavel?
e I'd like to .... from the guys in Ohio. — Are there any comments from Ohio?
f Let's .... where we are. — Let's review our progress.

5 Look at the sentences below describing good skills for leading virtual meetings. Match each of the words and phrases in bold with a similar word in the box.

| call | consensus | employ | engaged in | involve | motivate | reports |

a It is important to keep everyone **focused on** the topic in hand.
b Try to **include** each member of the team.
c **Encourage** quiet people to take their turn during discussion.
d Give verbal **commentaries** to explain what's happening.
e **Refer to** individuals by name.
f At critical points, ask everyone for **agreement**.
g **Use** a variety of different techniques to get responses from people.

6 Which of the skills listed in Exercise 5 do you feel most confident in?

Let's talk

7 a Take a few minutes to think about the last few meetings you participated in / facilitated. How focused were people? Write notes using these headings.

- types of meeting
- your role in the meetings
- examples of people being focused
- your lessons learned from these experiences

b Now share these experiences with the rest of the group.

D Intercultural competence: Thinking beyond the department

Departmental culture is the collective behaviour and beliefs of a group of people who work together. This collective behaviour is taught to new department members, and it affects the way people and groups interact with each other. More specifically, it affects the way knowledge is transferred by those who have it to those who need it. This can cause problems when cross-functional teams work together on a project.

1 What do you think are the main ways in which the culture of a department can be described? Brainstorm with a partner and add to this list.
   communication style
   way of working
   Relationship with others
   ...

2 What cultural differences do you see between departments in your organisation?

3 Discuss these questions.
   a What experience do you have of working on projects with people from other departments?
   b Do you normally communicate with each other face to face, or do you rely on other channels such as instant messaging or phone?
   c Which of these issues present the greatest challenge in your collaboration with other departments?
   - making contact with the right person (the one with the knowledge)
   - getting the right information
   - getting information on time
   - understanding/interpreting the information received

4 Look at this quote by Jeremy Comfort, author of *The Mindful International Manager*. How far do you agree with this statement?

> Individually, departments may be highly effective centres of expertise, but they may equally be little kingdoms, jealously guarded by their heads and insulated from positive outside influences. They get used to working autonomously, believing their way of working is the only way of working, and consequently, they're reluctant to transfer knowledge.

5 What can departments do to make collaboration between each other easier? Who should be responsible for encouraging effective knowledge transfer?

6 a Think about your department's culture and the way people collaborate with others. Are there any aspects of this culture which you would like to change?
   b Imagine that you and your colleague(s) have been asked to work on improving collaboration between departments. Identify the features of the culture you wish to focus on and prepare to present how you would bring about those changes to your department.

Case study: An issue with sharing information

Background A small group of highly skilled food technologists in the UK, working for a global confectionery company, have created an exciting new product which they are keen to move from the concept stage into production. They have been working closely with their colleagues from Production at one of the company's chocolate factories in Eastern Europe for the last six months and hope to have a new production line up and running in the next three weeks.

The food technologists feel that progress on the project has been slower than it should have been. They feel the Production team does not always understand what the food technologists want them to do – for example, in terms of converting the pilot trials into full-scale production. There is some tension between the two teams and, in addition, there also seems to be a problem with the interpretation of certain terminology. Consequently, the Production team has not yet come up with a line capable of producing the new product, and the project risks failing to meet its launch deadline.

Situation The Food Technologist team is becoming impatient with the frequent breakdown in communication and feels that the Production team is being deliberately obstructive. As project leader, Maxim knows that the project must move on to the next phase as a matter of urgency. This involves the Production team producing a set of plans for the production line by tomorrow. So far, Miloslav, his counterpart in Production, has done nothing but ask what Maxim feels are irrelevant questions about scientific terms. To Maxim, Miloslav seems obsessed with having definitions for everything.

Miloslav is used to dealing with clear instructions, specific deadlines and a set of standard definitions for processes. He finds Maxim's communications difficult to follow. He feels that food technologists use too many scientific terms with far too many abbreviations, and they expect everyone else to understand them. They don't seem to be able to transfer knowledge simply and clearly. Miloslav has a suspicious feeling that they are trying to make his team look stupid, so he will not ask them to explain what they mean.

The Food Technologist team regularly communicates with the Production team via instant messaging because they believe it is the easiest way to discuss problems and the quickest way to get results. Look at this typical exchange:

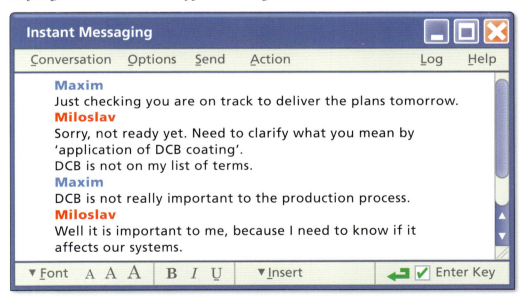

Task In groups, discuss these questions.

a What are the main factors preventing these two teams from working well together? What could they have done at the beginning of the project to make collaboration easier?

b What do you think the food technologists should do to improve relations between the two teams?

c How can the two teams work towards overcoming the differences in departmental cultures?

One person in each group should take notes on the discussion and give a short summary of the group's views.

E Language reference

Read through the key words and phrases below from this unit. Add any other useful words and expressions which you feel are important for you to learn. Make sure you find the time to review these words and phrases regularly and to use them at work.

Language summary
The four Ps of business communication
- Preparation
- Purpose
- Process
- People

Planning a virtual meeting

schedule / organise / set up a meeting	decide on timing
check differences in time zones	invite participants
draw up an agenda	decide on roles
circulate or distribute information	test the equipment

Leading a virtual meeting

state or outline the purpose	make/take decisions
establish rules or guidelines	ask for agreement
define aims and objectives	get consensus
present the context	review progress
control the time	request actions
handle turn-taking	

Interpersonal skills

encourage small talk	maintain relationships
put your audience at ease	keep people focused
build rapport	

Noun phrases

a channel of communication	a remote listener
a meeting platform	a web meeting
a mute button	virtual collaboration

Verbs and verb phrases

collaborate	include
doze off	multi-task
engage	pay attention
focus	raise hands

Meeting verbs and verb phrases

close	lead
facilitate	log in to
join	open
last	participate in

Functional phrases
Is that clear? / Does that make sense?
Christophe, do you have an opinion on this? / What do you think?
Would you give us a summary, David? / Can you sum up?
Can you take us through this point? / I'd like Angela to lead this point.
Could you present the next slide, Pavel? / Can you go through the next slide, Pavel?
I'd like to hear from the guys in Ohio. / Are there any comments from Ohio?
Let's look at where we are. / Let's review our progress.

Departmental cultures

collective behaviour	knowledge transfer
cross-functional teams	expertise

Writing task Choose one of these situations based on the case study. Try to include at least ten of the expressions from above in your e-mail.

1 Imagine you are Miloslav, the Production team leader. Write to Maxim, the Food Technologist team leader, explaining how you feel about the complex way he and his team work. Suggest how you can improve relations between the two teams.
2 Imagine you are Maxim. Write to the head of your department advising him/her that your current project is falling behind schedule and asking for an extension to the deadline. Explain the reason for the delay (you feel the Production team is to blame).

F Virtual working tips and personal action plan

1 Take a few minutes to reflect on these tips for preparing for virtual communication. Which do you think is the most important? Which ideas are the most useful?

TIP 1

Keep the four Ps in mind, when preparing for a conference call or an online presentation. Spend time planning your role in a meeting so the content and purpose is clear. Likewise, if your presentation is visually stimulating and the content and speed of delivery are suitable for your audience, they will maintain interest in your message.

Ideas for implementing the four Ps:
- Make sure that you have all the information in front of you, you are familiar with the technology and you have invited the relevant people.
- For presentations, think about number of slides and content. Practise in front of someone you can rely on to give you feedback on the clarity of your message.

TIP 2

As a facilitator, your greatest challenge is ensuring everyone understands what is going to happen. Outline the process clearly at the start and get people to agree communication norms.

Ideas for effective facilitation:
- Use phrases from this unit to help you manage the role of facilitator more effectively.
- Establish guidelines for group communication. Discuss the use of the mute button, how to address each other (e.g. by first names) and how to handle turn-taking and interruptions.
- If possible, record meetings. This helps minute-taking and lets you listen to and monitor your performance. Use it to evaluate your facilitation or participation.

TIP 3

Sending an e-mail may be the quickest and easiest way to communicate, but is it always the most appropriate? Think about how you communicate in different situations. Expressing feelings via e-mail or even phone is not always the best option.

Ideas for using the right communication channels:
- Experiment with a range of channels to improve your use of previously unfamiliar ways of communicating with groups or individuals. So, if you always use e-mail, pick up the phone instead!
- If you do write an e-mail, read it through before sending. Will it have the desired outcome?

---

2 What other ideas for preparing for virtual communication have you got from studying this unit?

Personal action plan 3 Think about what you have learned from this unit. Note down two or three important points which you want to apply to your own job (*What?*). Then create a schedule to implement your learning (*When?*) and think about the best way to check that you have successfully applied these ideas (*How?*).

4 Discuss your action plan and adapt it if necessary, based on any useful feedback you get.

	what I learned and want to apply to my job	when/how I will apply this in my job	how I will check if I have applied it
1			
2			
3			

2 Preparing for successful communication

3 Working in virtual groups

AIMS
A To lead conference calls effectively
B To develop language skills for conference calls
C To learn about success factors in virtual meetings
D To develop cross-cultural presentation skills

A Discussion and listening

Think about it

1 What is your experience of participating in or leading conference calls? How much of your working week do you spend on these calls?

2 How often do you finish a call feeling frustrated because of an unsatisfactory outcome? Give examples and suggest reasons.

Listen to this

3 🎧 **11** Listen to an interview with Karen Skelton, a product technology department head with Alimenton, a European-based food and drink producer. She has a lot of experience leading international projects with teams around the world. She discusses the logistics of conference calls (which she refers to as *telcos*). As you listen, answer these questions.

a According to Karen, why is it 'vital that things run smoothly'?
b Why could it be difficult for a factory manager to take part in a conference call?
c What is not usually discussed in conference calls?
d What is Karen's biggest challenge?

4 a 🎧 **12** Listen to the second part of the interview and decide whether each of these statements is true (T) or false (F).
   a The main objective of Karen's calls is to clarify the status of the project.
   b She thinks everyone should have a high level of English to participate.
   c Asian participants often ask people to repeat points during a call.
   d As a facilitator, Karen doesn't think she should say much during the call.
   e She encourages people to use language which is easy for everyone to understand.

b How important is a good language level in conference calls?

Focus on language

5 🎧 **12** Karen talks about a lot of competences needed to run a successful virtual meeting. Listen to the second part of the interview again and complete these sentences.
   a ... the main purpose is normally to .... everybody .... on the progress of a project ...
   b ... to .... important milestones have been reached ...
   c We need to .... an .... in which it's OK to admit you don't understand ...
   d ... to .... to use simple words ...
   e After all, it's about .... as simply as you can!

6 Match the sentence beginnings (1–7) with the endings (a–g) to make a short description of each competence.

1 Circulate the agenda
2 Communicate
3 Gather together
4 Check
5 Encourage
6 Discuss
7 Involve

a the right people at the right time.
b each participant fully.
c opinions fully.
d at least a day beforehand.
e there are no technology problems.
f ideas effectively.
g the use of simple language.

7 Read this 'to do' list for a busy virtual manager who needs to prepare for his weekly team meeting. Match each of the concepts from Exercise 6 with each of these action points.

> **NOTES TO SELF**
> i   Book teleconference suite, speak to tech. officer re: equipment (problems with sound last week).
> ii Send invites to dept. heads – choose participants.
> iii Make note – remind participants: no jargon!
> iv Write proper meeting notes – no improvising!!
> v   Make sure all get to speak equally (no dominators).
> vi Keep an eye on Luis – he often gets the wrong message.
> vii Agenda – copies to all pre-meeting.

Let's talk **8** Think about leading your virtual meetings. What do you find most challenging? In small groups, use this list to discuss the potential challenges when leading conference calls. Rank them in order of importance.
- Covering all the material on the agenda.
- People multi-tasking or not paying attention.
- Making necessary decisions.
- Establishing an action plan.
- Dealing with technical or communication issues.
- Getting everyone focused and participating.
- Keeping the meeting on track.
- Ease of use (and knowledge) of the technology platform.

9 You have a regular conference call, and the same issues arise very frequently. How would you deal with the following?

a Four of the eight participants are English native speakers. They tend to dominate, using very colloquial language, making 'in' jokes among themselves and speaking very fast. The other four participants (French, Japanese and two Spaniards) don't participate much.

b Two colleagues regularly ring in from their mobile phones. They are usually in traffic, using the 'hands-free' facility to drive and speak/listen. Other people don't comment, but a lot of time is used during the call asking the two people to repeat what they have said because of noise interference.

3 Working in virtual groups

B Communication skills: Language skills for conference calls

Think about it 1 Read these statements about working in virtual groups. Do you agree with any of them?

a I very much enjoy the ideas which are generated when you put people together to exchange best practice. Our calls are extremely positive and productive, and everyone gets involved.

b I find these calls very stressful if there are native speakers talking all the time. I'm not sure if I understand, and I never interrupt, but no one seems to notice.

c I believe that we could eliminate at least half the calls we take part in and exchange necessary information by e-mailing each other. I can't understand half of my colleagues, anyway!

d My weekly calls are a good opportunity for me to speak to all my team at once. We never see each other, so it's important for team spirit.

2 Look again at comments b and c in Exercise 1. What could you do to deal with the problems they highlight?

Listen to this 3 🎧 13 Identifying the speakers in a conference call can be a challenge in itself. You are going to listen to a call involving a company which produces bottled water for shops and supermarkets. A problem arises, and the call is arranged quickly to deal with it. There are five people involved. Listen to the opening part of the call and match the names of the participants from the box to their jobs below.

Imran Jessica ~~Richard~~ ~~François~~ Susana

1 Product Manager (head office) ......Richard...... (facilitator)
2 Communications Officer ....
3 Production Manager (at the plant) ....
4 Plant Manager ......François......
5 Quality Manager ....

4 🎧 13 Listen again. What is the subject of the call? What is the objective?

5 🎧 14 Listen to the end of the call and decide whether each of these statements is true (T) or false (F).
a Richard clarifies the action plan.
b The products need to be recalled from Spain and Poland.
c Susana (the Production Manager) isn't happy with the outcome of the call.
d Richard closes the meeting efficiently.

6 Is the conference call featured in Exercises 3–5 a good one? Why? / Why not?

'Teleconferencing makes it just like they're in the room with us – things are unclear and difficult to understand.'

Focus on language 7 🎧 **14** During the conference call, several of the participants use language to indicate the purpose of what they are saying. Listen again and complete these sentences.

a Richard, this is François. I .... what we're going to do about inventory in stores.

b Richard, ... , that means all regional distribution warehouses and retail outlets – points of sale – Benelux and Poland?

c I know you're all worried about this, but .... there's minimal risk of cross-contamination.

d Right. .... I just .... round and .... you're all .... with that?

e Jessica, you've been a bit quiet this morning. .... you .... the .... what's on your mind?

f That's obviously an important point, Imran, but .... you and I .... that .... the call?

8 The sentences below are more examples of language you can use to manage or participate in conference calls. Match each one with a purpose from the box.

| clarifying procedure | dealing with technology | finishing | getting feedback |
| inviting opinions | moving to next item | starting / welcoming participants |

a Can I ask everyone what they think of my proposal? Carlos, how do you feel?
   getting feedback

b I suggest we state our position on the issue and then discuss it more freely. Two minutes each, is that OK?

c Good afternoon, everyone, or good morning for Ramón! Thanks for being punctual.

d If you're OK with what we've done so far, let's move on to the next point.

e I think we've done what we can in the available time, so let's wrap things up.

f The connection is poor. Try logging off and re-joining the call.

g Can you all see the graph clearly? David, what do you think?

9 How many of the expressions in Exercise 8 do you use regularly to manage your virtual group tasks?

Let's talk 10 Work in groups of four. You are going to take part in a conference call. The information common to you all is below.

Organisational culture: background information

The executive board of your company has decided that there is a need to examine and improve the use of IT in the organisation. They have carried out research and made a list of proposals, which they would like you to discuss in more detail.

As you are very busy people, it is impossible to get you in the same place at the same time, so a conference call has been arranged to discuss the following items.

Agenda
1 Hardware replacement and modernisation
2 Software training

Student A (IT Manager):   Turn to page 88.
Student B (HR Manager):   Turn to page 90.
Student C (Sales Manager):   Turn to page 92.
Student D (Finance Manager):   Turn to page 94.

3 Working in virtual groups

C Professional skills: Success factors in virtual meetings

Think about it 1 How can people's behaviour affect the way we interact if we are not meeting face to face? What interpersonal factors does a call manager need to consider?

Read this 2 The text below is taken from a blog by an anonymous virtual team member. It describes good practice in virtual meetings. After reading the blog, decide whether each of these statements is true (T) or false (F).
   a The conference call itself covers half the total work.
   b If you invite a small number of participants, the result will probably be better.
   c It is better to use the mute button if there are other people talking in the room where you are.
   d It is good practice to hold international calls at the same time all the time.
   e It is not a good idea to introduce a variety of interaction in a conference call.

Quick tips for keeping virtual meetings focused and engaging

1 Start with clear objectives/outcomes. Effective meetings require careful planning, with stated objectives and outcomes – 80% of the work happens before the meeting begins.

2 Assign pre-work. Asking people to do a bit of homework, such as 'List three major challenges' or 'What do you hope to get from the session?' deepens commitment and encourages participation.

3 Invite as few people as possible. Often the most productive meetings have the fewest participants.

4 Arrange team meetings to foster teamwork and collaboration; build closer relationships by learning more about team members.

5 Keep hands off the mute button. Ask everyone to stay off mute unless there is too much background noise. People are much more likely to participate if they don't have to deal with their muting technology.

6 Level the playing field. Have everyone participate in meetings by phone, not split between face-to-face and virtual. Having mixed (virtual vs. face-to-face) participants creates first and second classes.

7 Avoid the tyranny of distance. Rotate meeting times so that all time zones get an equal share.

8 Pair technology and phone for greater productivity. Ask each person on a call to type comments, rather than say them. All can quickly see the combined results, which can then be discussed by the group.

9 Build multi-tasking into every meeting. Create activities that get participants typing. This can be done in a variety of ways – structured group exercises, electronic brainstorming, prioritising and voting.

3 Which section of the blog focuses on each of these managerial tasks?
   a ensuring equality of opportunity to participate
   b arranging suitable times for everyone
   c relationship-building
   d making participants do a task before the event
   e managing the number of people in the group

Focus on language

4 a Different kinds of language are used for managing conference calls, e.g. making suggestions, giving direction. Match these sentence beginnings (1–8) with the correct endings (a–h).

1 Each of you test your microphone
2 Why don't you turn up the sound
3 I think it's a better idea to start
4 OK. I want you all to present the
5 Let's write our ideas
6 I'd like you all to take a minute
7 Please don't talk amongst yourselves
8 All those participants not involved

a because otherwise, Jaume finds it all confusing.
b to introduce yourselves. OK?
c as messages so we can follow more easily.
d in the final decision can leave the call.
e so you can hear more clearly.
f at 09:00 CET next week, not 15:00.
g amendments you've made to the draft document.
h levels before we start, please.

b Decide if each of the completed sentences is *suggestion* or *direction*.
Example: 1 *direction*

5 Use your own ideas to complete these sentences.
a Multi-tasking is a good idea if you …
b If members of my virtual team are in different time zones, I will/can …
c If I want people to prepare for a conference call, I should …
d I need to state the objective clearly at the beginning of every call if I want …
e One way to get feedback at the end of the conference call is to …
f A good way for team members to get to know each other better is …

Let's talk

6 Look at the examples below of different types of behaviour during conference calls. In your organisation, is any of this behaviour common in virtual communication? Discuss with a partner which behaviour really annoys you and which is acceptable.

a Arriving late.
b Talking more than other participants.
c Interrupting people.
d Using humour and jokes.
e Avoiding saying 'No'.
f Praising and thanking other participants.
g Multi-tasking.
h Starting with an informal conversation.
i Speaking loudly.
j Being very brief and direct.

3 Working in virtual groups

D Intercultural competence: Cross-cultural presentation skills

> *Different cultures learn and take in information in varying ways. One should always try and tailor their (virtual) presentation style to meet the needs of the target culture.*
>
> www.kwintessential.co.uk

1 Look at the quote above. To what extent do you agree with it?

2 a Look at these factors which influence international virtual presentations. How challenging are they for you? Easy, quite challenging or very challenging?
- Presenting in a foreign language
- Not being able to use eye contact and non-verbal communication
- Keeping the whole audience engaged and interested
- Adapting your presentation style to meet different audience expectations

b Add some of your own challenges to the list and compare your results with a partner.

3 Here are two actual examples of self-presentation by members of international virtual teams.

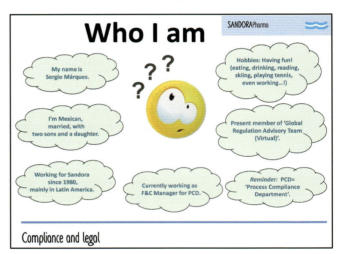

Bearing in mind the factors you looked at in Exercise 2, prepare a slide introducing yourself to international colleagues at a project kick-off meeting. Will you:
- speak informally with no visual material?
- introduce each piece of information separately or all at once?
- use humour?
- include information about your personal life? (If so, how much?)

4 Watch each other's virtual introductions and give feedback. Note any useful points to help you in the future.

Case study: Different international presentation styles

Background Marika East works for Konektion, a multinational telecoms corporation. She is a team member on a project developing new markets in Latin America. Marika regularly organises and attends international meetings. One of these is a project update meeting, which takes place every Monday morning and frequently runs over the finish time, sometimes lasting for over three hours. The project team is led by William Forest, based in the London office, and he facilitates the meeting. He usually books the tele-conference suite for two hours. In the meeting, each participant is required to give a fairly brief summary of the previous week's progress in their area. There are 12 team members: three from the Asia-Pacific region, five from Europe and four from Latin America.

Situation For several weeks, Marika has been unhappy about the Monday meetings. There is a wide variety of presentation styles used by different team members.
- Some complete their presentations well within the allotted time. Others can run over by as much as ten minutes.
- Some use slides, while others don't.
- Some have minimal information on their visual support, while others include as much text on each slide as possible.
- Some give very short, data-driven presentations, and do not seem to encourage questions.
- Some welcome questions and discussion during their presentations.
- Some are very time-conscious, but don't seem to be engaged in the meeting.

As a fairly new member of the project team, Marika is a little confused about how she should prepare and deliver her presentations. She is frustrated by the situation and is reaching the point where she doesn't want to attend the meetings.

Tasks 1 **In groups, discuss these questions.**
   a Do you think it is acceptable to encourage different presentation styles at the meeting?
   b To what extent is William Forest responsible for this situation?
   c Have you experienced similar situations in your virtual meetings? How were they handled?

2 **Draw up a short list of recommendations to present to the company in order to improve these meetings.**

E Language reference

Read through the key words and phrases below from this unit. Add any other useful words and expressions which you feel are important for you to learn. Make sure you find the time to review these words and phrases regularly and to use them at work.

Common expressions for group and individual tasks/objectives
transmit essential information, e.g. deliver project updates
air differences and synergies
(openly) discuss differences and difficult issues
celebrate achievements
coach underperforming/promising/high-potential team members
clarify issues / misunderstandings / exact meanings
share opinions/information/documents/desktops/applications

Starting off a virtual meeting
Welcoming people
Glad you could all make it!
Thanks for attending at such short notice.
It's good to have so many of you here today.
Hello, and welcome to our weekly update meeting.
Asking for introductions round the table
Could we just hear something briefly from everyone?
Can I ask everyone to say a few words about themselves?
Let's just spend a few minutes introducing ourselves, shall we?
When you don't hear someone clearly
Excuse me? / Pardon?
Could you say that again, Luis? The connection is bad.
I didn't catch that, Richard.
Abdul, I didn't hear (very well) what you said.
When you don't understand
Sorry, but I don't follow you, Heinz.
Helena, I don't (really/fully) understand your point.
Juan, can you expand on that?
Gilles, did you say 'healthy'?
Getting feedback
Carlos? How was today's meeting? Are you happy with all the decisions?
How good was everybody's understanding? Zhang Ying?
What could we do better next time?
How did you feel about the meeting?

Language for virtual presentations
Descriptive language for visual material
I want to highlight the trend on …
Note …
As you can see from …
I want to emphasise …
Looking at … , we can clearly see …

	this	graph,	you can see …
In	the following	flow chart,	on the left/right
	the	diagram,	at the top/bottom

Checking understanding and engagement
Can you all see that point?
Are you following me so far?
How does this chart look to you?
Any questions?
Maria, any thoughts/views/reflections/opinions about this?

Writing task Do both of these e-mail writing activities. Integrate at least ten of the words from above into your e-mails.
1 Look again at the Case study on page 35. Write an e-mail giving Marika advice.
2 At the start of a project, the team leader has asked each team member to send a short e-mail to everyone introducing themselves. Write an e-mail introducing yourself.

F Virtual working tips and personal action plan

1 Take a few minutes to reflect on these tips for preparing for virtual communication which arise in this unit. How far do you agree with each one? Which do you think is the most important, and which ideas are the most useful?

> **TIP 1**
> Before calling any meeting, make sure that you have clear, SMART objectives (S = Specific, M = Measurable, A = Attainable, R = Realistic, T = Time-bound). Write and distribute the agenda in advance, one or two days before the meeting, not just beforehand.
> Ideas for setting clear objectives:
> - Use a standard template for your agenda, so everyone knows how the call is structured.
> - Give yourself plenty of time to plan the agenda; you will look more efficient!

> **TIP 2**
> Make it clear to everyone that you always start and finish on time. Suggest they leave time either side of the meeting free to ensure punctuality. If that doesn't work, schedule it in for them. Time each item and allow for small delays, or you may not finish on time.
> Ideas for time-keeping:
> - Discuss the most important items first so if you run out of time, you do not leave significant material undiscussed. Think SMART about the time available.
> - Make it clear from the start what you expect from the group members in terms of time-keeping. Do you expect everyone to be there before the call is scheduled to start? Do they have a margin of five or ten minutes after the call starts?

> **TIP 3**
> Remember that in audio conferences, you can only express yourself using your voice and words. This may sound obvious – you have been doing it on the phone for years! However, working in groups requires changes in how you communicate, and the biggest change is making sure you state everything explicitly, especially attitudes, feelings and opinions.
> Ideas for adapting your communication style:
> - Use names as much as possible, not only when you offer your own opinions, but also when you address others. Using names increases clarity and focus.
> - Record yourself and listen to the volume of your voice. Problems with communication can often be as simple as not speaking loud enough or causing interference on the line by being too close to your microphone.

Personal action plan 2 Think about what you have learned from this unit. Note down two or three important points which you want to apply to your own job (*What?*). Then create a schedule to implement your learning (*When?*) and think about the best way to check that you have successfully applied these ideas (*How?*).

3 Discuss your action plan and adapt it if necessary, based on any useful feedback you get.

	what I learned and want to apply to my job	when/how I will apply this in my job	how I will check if I have applied it
1			
2			
3			

4 Working with technology

AIMS
A To look at trends in information communication technology (ICT)
B To evaluate the range of communication channels
C To choose technology for collaboration and engagement
D To reflect on cultural diversity and technology use

A Discussion and listening

Think about it 1 Which electronic communication devices do you use most? Why? Can you think of ways in which technology influences your communication in general?

2 Look at these words and phrases about trends in ICT. Discuss what each one means. Try to add more words and phrases referring to developments you know about.
- M-business
- tablet-computing
- voice recognition
- web-based apps
- the cloud
- virtual dashboards
- collaborative suites

Listen to this 3 🎧 **15–16** Listen to two professionals talking about trends in communication technology and complete the *development* column of this table with notes on the development that each person describes.

speaker	development	benefits
1 Rohan	virtual	• allows people to access live documents and edit them • • •
2 Birgitte	voice	• rapid response time • • •

4 What experience do you have of working with the technologies described in Exercise 3? What other technologies have you used?

5 🎧 **15–16** Listen again and complete the *benefits* column of the table in Exercise 3.

6 🎧 **17** Listen to the second part of the discussion and note the advantages or disadvantages that Rohan and Birgitte mention for each development.

7 Which development is (or could be) the most useful for you? Why?

Focus on language

8 🎧 **18** Rohan and Birgitte use common expressions to give their opinions and points of view. Listen and complete these sentences with the expressions they use.

    a B: So, Rohan, would you want to spend money on this product?
        R: I'm fascinated by virtual team boards and we .... they need to become standard practice for all our global teams!

    b R: Birgitte, how do you feel about larger business applications?
        B: I .... the future looks positive at all for large-scale software packages. .... they just aren't agile enough, especially for small and medium-sized businesses.

    c R: So, Birgitte, do you think this voice-recognition software will become standard?
        B: Well, to be honest, I'm .... that the busy business executive can use this software safely to send out directions and orders – human beings make mistakes!

    d R: Are we going to see the end of the written word, Birgitte?
        B: I .... people who say voice recognition eliminates the need for e-mailing – the writing process makes you think twice about the message you are sending.

9 Look at the sentences below (a–e) and match each one with the strength of opinion it expresses (1–5).

Example: *a 2*

1 strong positive opinion
2 positive opinion
3 speculation/uncertainty
4 negative opinion
5 strong negative opinion

    a I think we should involve all the markets in this decision – it impacts on them all.
    b As far as I'm concerned, networking all these desktops is out of the question.
    c I don't think we should rush into making a decision.
    d She's totally convinced about implementing this strategy in the Russian market.
    e I agree up to a point that he's the right person for the position, but I need to see his quarterly results.

Let's talk

10 a Look at the five statements below (a–e) and, for each one, choose one of these standpoints to base your views on. Choose a different standpoint for each statement.

- strongly agree
- partly agree
- neither agree nor disagree
- partly disagree
- strongly disagree

    a We would all save lots of time by avoiding conference calls and just communicating via e-mail or other written channels.
    b Internet communication is destroying the ability to interact face to face.
    c Cross-cultural miscommunication is why virtual teams often perform badly.
    d About 80% of the work e-mails we receive are of no value.
    e There is no need for chatting or socialising when working virtually.

    b Work in groups. Discuss the statements using expressions of opinion from Exercise 9 and others of your own.

B Communication skills: The range of communication channels

Think about it

1 Think about the different communication channels now used in business (e.g. the phone). Choose one of them and discuss its main advantages and disadvantages for business communication.

Listen to this

2 a You are going to hear Alan Roberts, a consultant, talking about different types of virtual communication and the hardware we use with them. Before you listen, look at these statements and decide whether you think each one is true (T) or false (F).
   a Mobile devices allow us to carry out only simple tasks.
   b Technological advances mean we can increase the quantity of data we send.
   c Some parts of the world have difficulties with the reliability of their connection.
   d The cost of technology is not a significant factor.
   e Using technology significantly changes the way people communicate.

b 🎧 19 Now listen to Alan and check your answers.

3 Look at these two definitions:

> • **synchronous:** occurring at the same time; simultaneous
> • **asynchronous:** not occurring at the same time. Each task or activity starts only after the preceding operation is completed.

Decide whether each of these communication channels is synchronous (S) or asynchronous (AS).
a VoIP   b audio conferencing   c teleconferencing   d blog posting
e instant messaging   f e-mailing   g telephoning   h application-sharing
i sharing desktops   j delivering or attending webinars

4 🎧 20 Listen to the second part of the interview and complete this diagram as Alan describes it.

5 🎧 20 Listen again to Alan's response to the interviewer's final question and answer this question.
How does Alan make the distinction between simple collaboration and complex collaboration?

6 Discuss with a partner whether each of these utterances is an example of simple or complex collaboration.
   a Can we brainstorm some options?
   b Send me that updated report, will you?
   c Hi, Dave. I need the access code for the CMS database.
   d Do you have time for a chat about your target attainment?
   e So, Azra, can you start with your update, then we'll move onto Frank's.
   f Daniela, can I ask you a quick question about the agenda for tomorrow's meeting?

Focus on language **7** Match each phrase on the left (1–8) with one on the right (a–h) to form expressions related to work we can do using technology.

   1 Upload sales figures   a your secure user account.
   2 Stream video   b for new versions.
   3 Automatically update   c to a recording of a conference call.
   4 Track and monitor   d to cloud-based storage space.
   5 Install web-based   e social-media traffic.
   6 Back up data   f for access by colleagues.
   7 Send a link   g to a telepresence suite.
   8 Remotely access   h applications.

8 Complete each of these sentences using the correct form of an expression from Exercise 7.
   a You couldn't join the call? I'll .... a .... to a .... of the .... so you can see what we discussed.
   b If you're a customer-facing department, it's critically important to .... and .... your ....-............... .... to see what the public are saying about you.
   c We no longer have large software suites on our servers. It's much more efficient to ....-............... .... which best respond to our specific requirements and which are cheaper to use!
   d If you want to .... your .... account from overseas, you need a card-reading device.
   e If we need to .... much more data than usual, we simply rent more space on the server for that month, because our ....-............... data storage capacity is scaleable* and flexible.
   f Our sales staff can .... their .... to a remote server, which means colleagues can .... that information wherever they are and whenever they want.

   * Can be made bigger or smaller according to requirements

Let's talk **9** Successful virtual work requires a suitable environment, which means optimising opportunities for effective communication. Many large organisations use software suites containing all the technological elements necessary for a variety of purposes.
Below are examples of some of the communication tools now available. With a partner, consider how you could improve, change or add to the tools you use.
   - conference-calling software with large range of functionalities
   - internal messaging software
   - data storage (content management)
   - task-based mobile applications
   - 'diary' system for availability
   - individual dashboards for virtual teams
   - virtual CRM
   - e-learning modules
   - project tools (diaries, timelines, milestones, etc.)

10 Would people's personal preferences influence your decisions? Why? / Why not?

4 Working with technology

C Professional skills: Choosing technology for collaboration and engagement

Think about it 1 What technological factors do you need to think about if you want everyone to work together effectively? How can you use technology to keep everyone involved?

Read this 2 Read the opening section of a blog post and answer the questions below.

> **What's a collaboration suite and why should you care?**
> *Laurie McCabe*
> For me, if your business is suffering from collaboration chaos, the common warning signs often include:
> 1 Too much time wasted on missed phone calls, searching for missing phone numbers and locating people with the know-how you need.
> 2 Bottlenecks in finding information or resources needed to get a job done.
> 3 E-mail overload and 'multiple version' issues, such as trying to figure out which version of a document is the most recent one.
> 4 Mistakes made because people are using incorrect or outdated information.
> 5 An overload of customer-service calls.
> 6 Delays in decision-making because people can't access and/or agree on what the 'right' information is.

Which of the problems mentioned involve:
a inconsistencies in storage of written data?
b an excessive quantity of requests?
c a delay in completing a task or job because of poor information flow?
d information which is out of date?
e using time inefficiently to find colleagues or missing information?
f arguing over the quality of information?

3 Read the rest of the blog below and answer these questions.
a What is unnecessary when you start to use the suite?
b What is the payment system for these suites?
c What can you do if you are not sure you want to start paying immediately for a suite?
d What does the expression *on the same page* mean?
e Why do small businesses need to adapt to a new environment?
f What are the main qualities of the suites, according to the blogger?

> These suites mean you don't need to buy, install or configure any hardware or software, or hire IT staff or consultants to get things up and running. You simply log in via a web browser to buy and use the service, which is typically sold through a monthly or annual per-user subscription, with a certain amount of e-mail storage included as part of the subscription price. Collaboration-suite vendors offer free trials, so you can try before you buy.
>
> **Why should you care?**
> Collaboration is probably the only activity that everyone in every company engages in every day. We all need to share and manage information, ideas, resources and connections to get our job done. Effective collaboration tools help you to share knowledge, streamline processes and keep everyone in the organisation 'on the same page'.
> Until recently, most small businesses could get along just fine with a few tools, such as e-mail, calendars, document sharing and the good old telephone. But in the last few years, the growth of digital information has been exponential. At the same time, the kinds of device we use to collaborate – from desktops to notebooks to smartphones to tablets – have exploded. Online collaboration suites integrate many pieces of the collaboration puzzle into a unified solution that makes it easier to find, share, manage and use information, and to locate and connect with the people you need when you need them.
>
> adapted from www.smallbusinesscomputing.com

4 What is your experience of using collaboration suites? If you haven't yet used one, would you find it useful? Share your experience and ideas with a partner.

Focus on language

5 There are usually rules and guidance concerning how company technology is used. Complete the e-mail below to a new employee from the IT department, using the words and phrases in the box.

| access | application | coverage | filter | firewall | incident ticket | log-on |
| operating | password | remote | reserve | spam | tablet | volume |

From: Jens Lehmann, IT
To: Marie Storey
Subject: Project review

Dear Marie,
As you have just joined us, here are a few instructions about norms for use of our systems at Davis Corp.
Firstly, we have recently changed our **(a)** .... system, so if you're having problems, you need to exit the **(b)** .... and log in again.
If you have a problem hearing other people during conference calls, open the control panel and check the **(c)** .... levels on your headphone set.
Incidentally, don't forget that in certain parts of our Central American market, **(d)** .... is limited, so you can expect a poor-quality line at certain times when there is a lot of traffic.
If you fail to **(e)** .... the network more than twice, you need to contact Renny and ask him for a new **(f)** .... The **(g)** .... protecting our internal network will **(h)** .... all mail and prevent any **(i)** .... getting through.
Unless you **(j)** .... it in good time, you'll find it impossible to use the teleconference suite, so I'd book it a week ahead if I were you.
Wherever you are, you have **(k)** .... access to your account using your **(l)** .... device. It generates a random PIN each time.
Finally, remember, if you have any hardware problems, you need to fill in an **(m)** .... for IT support so they can provide you with a replacement laptop or **(n)** .... as soon as possible.
Let me know if you need any more information. Good luck!
Kind regards,
Jens

Let's talk

6 Discuss these statements in small groups and exchange your experiences.

a IT helpdesks never teach you how to solve a problem – they keep that to themselves.

b If the majority of a virtual team decides on procedures and a minority disagrees with them, the majority view wins.

c Software training in large companies is badly designed and too generic.

d We should never turn off our work phones because important messages arrive 24/7.

e Technological developments are too far ahead of our ability to use them well.

'I like the touch screen, but I miss playing with the mouse.'

4 Working with technology

D Intercultural competence: Cultural diversity and technology use

1 How can the choice of communication channels affect how people from different cultures work together? Are some channels more suited to particular situations?

2 This diagram identifies the quality and 'richness' of communication depending on the media used.

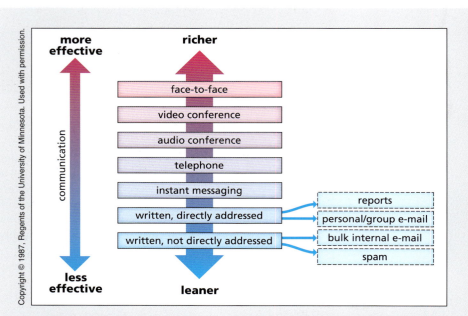

So-called 'lean' mediums are not good for indicating the communication we take for granted in everyday face-to-face interactions – they do not clearly convey our feelings, intentions or sense of humour. However, when the message is relatively simple to understand, they are quick and efficient. When we want to communicate more complex messages, where emotion and attitude form part of the impact, a 'rich' communication channel will be more effective. Increasingly sophisticated technology makes it somewhat easier for recipients to interpret voice. Video-conferencing allows participants to view non-verbal communication. Certain larger organisations even use online virtual worlds – 3D environments in which colleagues, using avatars, adopt the 'norms' of real-world behaviour. As tablet devices become the norm, video conversations are no longer confined to a fixed place, and can help to make the interaction more authentic and personal.

Using information from the diagram and text, discuss and decide which would be the best communication channel to deal with these situations.
a Informing someone they no longer have a job with your organisation.
b Asking someone to clarify factual information they gave in an earlier conversation.
c Asking someone to elaborate on an opinion they expressed in an earlier conversation.
d Conveying important new information to a number of different colleagues.
e Introducing and welcoming a new colleague who is joining an ongoing project.

3 Work in small groups. What channel(s) of communication would you use for these situations?
a Presenting an advertising campaign proposal to a marketing team from a US oil company based in Texas.
b Working on a specific detail in a joint project with an R&D department for a Swedish engineering company.
c Clarifying a problem with the export department of a packaging company in Chile.
d Getting a project status update from a team of 25 software programmers and designers based in Delhi.

Case study: The virtual inbox

Background Hans Blick leads a team of managers running local back-office finance support for various markets around the world. Generally, the team runs smoothly, but at times there are problems with lack of local standardisation, and conflicting interests between local line managers and the global interests of the company. Hans is trying to move away from the 'hand-holding' culture of the team which seems to have emerged over its short lifetime. He wants each team member to develop less reliance on him as a troubleshooter and learn to solve immediate problems with greater autonomy.

Situation While Hans was away on a short trip overseas for personal reasons, his briefcase was stolen, leaving him out of contact with work for several hours. Once he managed to replace his phone, he found texts, e-mails and voicemail messages requiring his attention. The messages are shown below in the order Hans received them.

 1 Hans, Guillem not responding to mails. Action? Sam

 2 Hans, We got a response from San Francisco and it looks like they need more validation tests. When can we convene the tech team for a meeting? I suggest ASAP!! Lisa

 3 Hi Hans. Lisa copied me into her mail about San Francisco. I told her two weeks ago that they wouldn't be happy with the validation as it stands. Can you have a word asap?

 4 21

 5 Hi Hans, hope you're OK. I was copied into a mail from Lisa to you about the Yanks. It's a bit short notice for a meeting on validation tests, isn't it? We're right in the middle of another process, and it's not going to be easy to just stop that. Anyway, you'll get back to me, yeah? I've copied Lisa in just so she knows I've been in touch with you. Wenshui

 6 Can't reach you by e-mail. Wenshui copied me into the mail he sent you. Typical of him to go over my head. Not the first time, either. Could we sort this testing thing out? Where are you, anyway? Lisa

 7 22

 8 23

 9 Hans! Why haven't you answered?! Guillem's been on the phone to me with some strange story about local suppliers refusing to deliver because we haven't conformed to terms ... I've no idea what's going on, but whatever it is, he doesn't seem to be able to cope with it. I really need a steer from you on this, Hans.

Tasks 1 **Using the information above, decide which issues Hans has to deal with.**

2 **Discuss how to prioritise the action required for each issue.**

3 **Discuss and decide on a response (where necessary).**

E Language reference

Read through the key words and phrases below from this unit. Add any other useful words and expressions which you feel are important for you to learn. Make sure you find the time to review these words and phrases regularly and to use them at work.

Virtual communication software and tasks

to send a blind copy / bcc
audio conferencing
video conferencing
teleconferencing
instant messaging

webinars / to deliver/attend a webinar
desktop-sharing / to share your desktop
to copy someone into (a message) / cc
application-sharing / to share applications

Synchronous: VoIP, audio conferencing, teleconferencing, instant messaging, telephoning, application-sharing, sharing desktops, delivering/attending webinars
Asynchronous: blog posting, e-mailing, instant messaging

Verbs for touchscreen technology
click on (an icon / an underlined/highlighted word)
drag (the icon / the file)
drag and drop (an icon / a file / a document)
position (the cursor)
scroll down/up (a screen)
swipe (up/down/left/right)
tap (a key / a mousepad)
press (the on/off button)

Technology verbs
access / log into (a network)
back-up (versions/copies/files/documents)
install / uninstall (software/apps/anti-virus/firewalls)
save / save as / delete (a file / a document type)
stream (video/audio)
track/monitor (social media traffic / progress / tasks)
update (files/versions/documents/colleagues/programs)
upload/download (documents / sales figures / files)

Expressing opinions
I totally agree with …
I (really) like the idea of … (-ing)
I couldn't agree more!
On the one hand, … , (but) on the other (hand), …
I'm in two minds whether/about …
I'm not (entirely) sure about/if …
I agree up to a point, but …
We're not (so/really) sure if/whether …
I don't see the point in … (-ing)
(As far as I'm concerned,) … is out of the question.

Addressing problems with technology
Can you all hear me OK?
Can you log out and in again and see if that helps?
Can you move a little closer to the microphone?
The connection is bad. Could you dial in again?
Call the IT helpline/hotline/helpdesk.

Writing task Choose one of these e-mail writing activities. Integrate at least ten of the words from above into the e-mail of your choice.
1 Your manager has asked you to send a short e-mail to a new team member explaining how to use a particular application on the team virtual dashboard. Write a short set of specific instructions.
2 In Section B, Exercise 9, you decided on the elements to include in your virtual office. Your line manager has asked for a brief summary of the decisions you made (and reasons). Write a brief report outlining those decisions and the costs involved.

F Virtual working tips and personal action plan

1   Take a few minutes to reflect on these tips for preparing for virtual communication which arise in this unit. How far do you agree with each one? Which do you think is the most important, and which ideas are the most useful?

TIP 1
Choose the best channel for the best communication; in general, the more personal and sensitive the issue, the 'richer' the communication channel needs to be. This means using video, phone calls and face-to-face meetings to communicate on more complex and human-oriented subjects requiring agreement, persuasion or coaching. For process-based and simple communication tasks, the channel can be 'lean' – e-mail, instant messaging or even a posting on a team board if there are multiple recipients.
Ideas for choosing channels:
- Try to establish agreement with the people you communicate with about how you will contact each of them. Be consistent about your use of different channels.
- Agree as a group which channels are appropriate for which tasks. If possible, discuss this before you get into a situation where different people are using different channels, to avoid confusion.

TIP 2
Instant messaging is not just used for making quick enquiries or solving simple problems rapidly. IM can also be used for collaborative tasks and even feedback, where the correspondent(s) may feel more comfortable communicating in written form.
Ideas for using instant messaging:
- As an alternative to a phone call, try using instant messaging when you know the other person is available.
- Encourage people to use instant messaging as a way of asking for clarification during a conference call, when details or data may be unclear to them.

TIP 3
When using technology, there is specific language and terminology needed (for example, dealing with problems or giving and receiving instructions). You will save a lot of time if you can correctly use the right verb or term for the action you require. For help, refer to Section E on page 46.
Ideas for use of terminology:
- Make sure everyone is aware of the latest developments and uses of the technology you have available. Members of virtual teams do not always keep up to date with the range of options they have. A periodic information update is useful for everyone.
- Different international coleagues may have different terms for certain technology, so prepare a 'glossary' of the language you use.

Personal action plan   2   Think about what you have learned from this unit. Note down two or three important points which you want to apply to your own job (*What?*). Then create a schedule to implement your learning (*When?*) and think about the best way to check that you have successfully applied these ideas (*How?*).

3   Discuss your action plan and adapt it if necessary, based on any useful feedback you get.

	what I learned and want to apply to my job	when/how I will apply this in my job	how I will check if I have applied it
1			
2			
3			

5 Effective writing

AIMS
A To develop a process for writing effectively
B To learn how to be clear and concise
C To choose the right content and technical level
D To consider cultural differences in writing

A Discussion and listening

Think about it **1** Which types of written communication do you use most often (e-mail, report, instant messaging)? Who do you write to, and how often? What are the main reasons for writing?

2 Read these comments made by native and non-native speakers and answer the questions below.

A I don't always know how to address the recipient. It often depends on cultural issues, personality or even organisational status.

B I like using IM to communicate with my team, but sometimes it's difficult to get the right message across, especially if I want someone to do something urgently. I'm afraid of sounding impolite.

C I find it difficult to say exactly what I mean in a short space. When I read my e-mails back, they're too long, and the message is not always as clear as I'd like.

D Sometimes I get copied into chains of e-mail correspondence and I don't know whether I'm supposed to reply or not.

a Which comments could have been made by non-native speakers?
b What are the biggest challenges that non-native speakers face when writing in English?
c Which of the above comments do you identify with most? Share your experiences with a partner.

Listen to this **3** 🎧 **24** Listen to three postgraduate students preparing to write their doctorates. They are discussing how to write more effectively. Then answer these questions.
a What are the four different steps of the process that Virginia and Yashi talk about?
b What does Virginia say about collecting information?
c What does Yashi say about how different people like to receive information?
d What should a writer avoid doing?
e How can a writer make their writing flow?

4 🎧 **24** Listen again and complete these phrases.
a … then make sure you have all the facts at ....
b … others prefer a softer, more .... style.
c … too much technical ....
d Keep your writing short and ....
e Try to have a .... of long and short sentences …

5 Which parts of the writing process discussed by the three students do you think are the most important? Why?

Focus on language **6** These six steps outline the basic process for writing efficient e-mails.
1 Plan the content.
2 Consider your reader.
3 Structure the information.
4 Choose the correct language.
5 Check what you have written.
6 Send the document.

Complete the steps in this flow chart using the words in the box on the left.

collect
content
edit
language
recipient

Take time to **(a)** .... relevant information before you write.

⬇

Think about the **(b)** .... How will they react?

⬇

Structure the **(c)** .... clearly and logically.

⬇

Select the right **(d)** .... Make sure it's not too technical.

⬇

Write a draft, check it and **(e)** .... if necessary.

7 In Exercise 3, one of the students talked about the need for a clear purpose when writing. Match each of the opening phrases (a–l) with a reason for writing (1–6). There are two phrases for each reason.

1 inviting
2 apologising
3 requesting
4 complaining
5 informing
6 thanking

a I'm writing to ask if you could …
b Just to let you know that …
c Many thanks for …
d I am writing to complain about …
e Would you like to …?
f Please accept our apologies for not …
g Could you …?
h Sorry for …
i We are not happy about …
j Please note the following …
k We would like to ask you …
l I really appreciate …

8 Write your own endings for these opening phrases.
a Just to let you know that *I am on holiday from Monday 12 July*.
b I am writing to complain about …
c Would you like to …?
d Many thanks for …
e Sorry for …
f I'm writing to ask if you could …

9 a Look at phrases a–f in Exercise 8 again and decide which ones are formal and which ones are less formal.
b Does your company or organisation prefer a formal or an informal style of writing? Are there any guidelines or models which you should follow?

Let's talk **10** Writing is not always the most appropriate channel for communication, especially if the message content is very complex. Work in pairs or small groups and turn to page 88.

5 Effective writing

B Communication skills: Being clear and concise

Think about it

1 How often do you receive an e-mail which is not clear? What can make e-mails unclear?

2 With a partner, brainstorm a list of important features of a good e-mail. Compare your list with other pairs. Do you agree? If not, why not?

Listen to this

3 🎧 25 A small group of consultants responsible for recommending innovation projects in a large multinational drinks company is finding communication with senior management a real challenge. They are meeting Robert, a communication expert, to brainstorm ways of solving this problem. Listen to their discussion and answer these questions.
   a What does Sanjeev say about the current relationship with senior management?
   b What solution does Robert suggest?
   c What would Mika like to focus on most?

4 What other elements of writing do you think should be included in this training in order to help the consultants to improve their communication with senior management?

Focus on language

5 In Exercise 3, the communication expert recommends using sentence connectors to make writing more effective. Match each of the connectors below (1–11) with its function (a–e). One connector has more than one function.
Example: 1 d

a addition   b cause   c contrast   d conclusion   e sequence

1 in conclusion   2 furthermore   3 however   4 therefore   5 in addition
6 consequently   7 yet   8 although   9 finally   10 so   11 next

6 Join these pairs of sentences in a way that makes sense using the more appropriate connector of the two given in brackets.
   a The meeting was badly organised. No one seemed to know who was leading it. (*therefore / in addition*)
   b We have now missed the deadline for phase 1. The project is no longer on schedule, and we will have to work much faster. (*consequently / in conclusion*)
   c Many of the participants are unable to attend the teleconference. I have decided it is better to postpone it for a week. (*therefore / furthermore*)
   d There has still been no improvement in team communication. Ben has arranged a team-building activity for next Monday. (*however / so*)
   e I thought my instructions were very clear. People are still not using the template which was sent out last month. (*furthermore / yet*)
   f I would prefer to discuss this point at a later date. This is not possible. (*finally / however*)
   g I'm writing to let you know that no decision has been made on the new staff restaurant yet. We have had some very interesting suggestions from employees. (*although / in addition*)

7 Complete these sentences using your own words.
   a I'm not happy with what I've written in this report, so …
   b Everyone in the meeting was clearly confused by what David what saying; however, …
   c Although she is an excellent team leader, …
   d Working across different time zones can be difficult; furthermore, …
   e In addition to the figures already provided, we require …

8 The e-mail extract below is from a product manager about a marketing plan. Complete it using suitable linking words or expressions from the box.

| as a result of | firstly | however | in addition | next | therefore |

Dear Yulia

(a) .... a recent meeting with the Marketing Department, I have drawn up the following revised marketing plan, which I am sure will be of interest to you. This plan will be implemented over the next nine months, beginning with a full-scale market survey. Obviously, this needs to be an in-depth survey, covering as wide a section of the population as possible. (b) .... , we will carry this out in two separate stages, starting in the north of the country, followed by south. (c) .... we will collect the results and analyse them. This may take up to three months; (d) .... , we expect to get some useful data. This data will enable us to define the new product range, but (e) .... we will need to develop the prototypes. (f) .... , we will have to gather a team of specialists to test these prototypes. This is where you come in. I'd like you to be responsible for selecting these specialists.

Let's talk 9 Look at these comments about written communication made by members of a team. In small groups, discuss how the team leader could advise them on their attitude to writing.

- I don't read any e-mail that is cc-ed to me.
- I think a member of my team is dyslexic – either that or he didn't study spelling at school!
- She needs to be more transparent in writing, rather than trying to be so polite to her colleagues.
- His written style is so brief that's it's telegraphic – I can't get any real meaning out of it.
- If she puts another of those smileys at the end of a message to me, I'll scream!
- I only read the executive summary and the recommendations. I haven't time for the rest.
- I delete anything that takes me more than 15 seconds to skim-read.

Possible questions which could be raised during discussion:
- How important is it to read all e-mails you receive? How can you filter them?
- Should a leader send out a style guide to all team members?
- If so, what should it include? Run a spell check after writing all e-mails? No use of emoticons?
- How long should it take you to read an e-mail? Is there a maximum acceptable length?
- Should you use complete sentences when writing e-mails? Or is it OK to write in note form?
- Who decides what is 'polite' and what is not?
- What are the dangers of skim-reading, or not reading a complete document?

C Professional skills: Choosing the right content and technical level

Think about it

1 Does your company or department use specialist terms or abbreviations in written communication? How easy is it for those outside your department to understand these terms?

2 How sensitive are you to your reader's technical knowledge? What can you do to minimise the effort needed by your reader to understand your writing?

Read this

3 Read this extract from the Plain English website, which outlines the benefits of writing in clear, simple language. Then decide whether the statements below are true (T) or false (F).

The Plain English checklist

Almost anything – from leaflets and letters to legal documents – can be written in plain English without being oversimplified. It doesn't mean reducing the length of your message or changing its meaning. Most of the UK's biggest insurance companies produce policies that explain everything fully in plain English.

It is not about banning new words, killing off long words or promoting completely perfect grammar. Nor is it about forgetting grammar altogether.

It's not an amateur's method of communication. Most forward-looking senior managers always write in plain English.

And finally, it's not as easy as we would like to think. Sadly, thanks to the bureaucrats of public-service industries, local councils, banks, building societies, insurance companies and government departments, we have learned to accept an official style of writing that is inefficient and often unfriendly.

a Plain English means writing short sentences.
b Certain words are banned by the Plain English website.
c We have all learned to accept the bureaucratic style of written documents.

4 The e-mail on page 53 was sent by Francesco Puttinelli, an Italian IT manager, to the HR and Payroll departments in the multinational company he works for. The IT department has been working for a long time on a project to standardise the payroll system, but some of the countries involved are not respecting the procedure which Francesco has set up. He is beginning to lose patience and has sent the e-mail in an attempt to improve the situation. Read it and answer these questions.

a What is the purpose of the e-mail?
b What is the problem?
c How does Francesco intend to monitor the current situation?
d What does Francesco threaten to do?

> Dear all,
>
> I have been doing an audit on the system and have found that you are still configuring your payroll data using the HR Dev system (GZ12). This is something which I have previously asked you not to do.
> Consequently, there are a few things I need to clarify ASAP to avoid negative impact for other markets / other areas (e.g. FICO, ERP Upgrade):
> 1 I have seen that monthly salary figures are calculated using the GCCR value and then converted with RM. This is too complicated.
>   GCE already has a process in place for PY & TM config. for those payroll departments operating in Italy, Spain and France. You need to follow the same process!
> 2 Why do you create bank data in V_T015 (GZ5K906985)? This data should be configured in FICO and transferred to HR via INTERLINK!
>
> We will closely check all the configurations you do from now on and request regular feedback from HQ to check whether you are making the transition away from the current 'non-process' to a structured and standard way of working.
> If we don't see a change in the way the configuration is handled, then we will remove your configuration rights.
>
> Best regards,
>
> Francesco

5 With a partner, read the e-mail again and discuss these questions.
   a Is the quantity of information appropriate? If not, what recommendations would you make?
   b How could Francesco improve the structure of the e-mail?
   c What is the effect of using a lot of abbreviations?
   d How do you think the recipients felt when they read the e-mail?
   e Do you think Francesco should have arranged a meeting to discuss this matter instead of sending an e-mail? Why? / Why not?

6 Which points in Francesco's e-mail do you think are the most essential to the reader?

Focus on language **7** E-mails which are short and clear will often be more effective than long, complex ones. Using a verb rather than a noun is one way to make sentences shorter and easier to read. Make each of these sentences shorter using a verb rather than a noun.
   a The company made the decision to outsource its cleaning contract.
      The company decided to outsource its cleaning contract.
   b His team leader made an announcement that overtime was no longer allowed.
   c We gave them permission to use our photos for publicity.
   d They made several recommendations on energy reduction in their report.
   e Everyone made a comment on the new canteen.
   f I prefer to make a phone call than to send an e-mail.
   g May I make a suggestion that we look for alternative suppliers?

Let's talk **8** With a partner, think about what you have learned in this unit. Describe to each other briefly what your main challenges are when writing e-mails. Then give each other tips on how you can both improve your writing skills.
Use this framework to note down your partner's recommendations to you, in order to create an action plan for future writing.

challenge	recommendation/action
My sentences are too long.	

5 Effective writing

D Intercultural competence: Cultural differences in writing

1 Look at these two e-mails. In pairs or small groups, discuss and make a note of any differences in style. Which e-mail do you prefer? Why?

A
> Dear Mr Pisarro
> I hope you are well and that business is good. I would like to make an appointment with you in order to discuss the new guidelines for carrying out credit checks on new customers. I would be grateful if you could let me know if you are available to discuss this matter next week, preferably on Monday or Tuesday.
> Best wishes

B
> Dear Ms Kunzel
> I hope you are well and that business is good. I have a question about your company's credit rating which I hope you will be able to clarify. As I understand the situation, it appears you may not have the required rating to enable us to supply you with goods on credit. If this is the case, I would like to point out that our company has a strict policy regarding payment terms for new customers. The full details are in our credit agreement, a copy of which is attached. (For your convenience I have highlighted the relevant clauses.) I would be grateful if you could get back to me and confirm that these guidelines are being followed. Of course, if you have any questions on this matter, or any other, please do not hesitate to contact me.
> With best wishes

2 Discuss these questions in pairs or small groups.
  a Which e-mail is easier to read? Why?
  b In e-mail B, the writer includes a lot of background detail. Why do think they do this?
  c Which e-mail is more focused on the task?
  d In your company, do people tend to write in a style similar to e-mail A or e-mail B? Are there any company guidelines or templates which you follow when writing e-mails in English?

Case study: The right message?

Background Tim (British) and Janine (Australian) are both leaders of small teams which are part of a much bigger multinational team across five continents. They have never met, but have been involved in several projects together in the past. They have always communicated with each other exclusively by e-mail because of the time difference and working hours.

Situation The current project is drawing to a close, but there are some important tasks which have yet to be completed. Deadlines are approaching, and Tim is anxious to find out what is going on. He had a progress meeting with Phil, a relatively new and inexperienced member of his team in Kuala Lumpur, and returned to London worried. He drafted the first e-mail on page 55 to Janine.

> Dear Janine,
> I hope things are going well at your end. I know there are lots of exciting things in the pipeline!
> I've just got back from KL, where I met with Phil. As I'm sure you know full well, he's got an incredibly heavy workload at present, and he seemed to me to be tired and demotivated.
> We both know Phil's seen as high-potential material, but he appears to be unhappy with the present situation, so I was wondering how you felt about it. Do you feel you both have a satisfactory working relationship with him?
> I do appreciate the tough schedule you have, but I got the impression he felt you don't appreciate the pressure he is under. I told him I would contact you so you could talk it over and get things off your chests.
> How do you feel about that? When all's said and done, we're going to work together much more effectively if we're working in a mutually supportive environment.
> I realise it's difficult when we hardly ever see each other and I do appreciate the stresses you are under, so if you want to talk, give me a call. If I'm not there, I'll get back to you as soon as I possibly can.
>
> Best regards,
> Tim

Before sending the e-mail, Tim decided to reread it. On reflection, he felt that Australians probably respond better to a more direct approach. So he changed his style, rewrote the message in a more straightforward way and sent it to Janine.

> Dear Janine
> I have just got back from KL, where I met with Phil. As Phil's zone manager, I was surprised at how demotivated Phil has become. As you know, he is regarded by me and others as high potential. He is very polite, but it is clear that he has found working with you difficult.
> I understand the pressure you are under at your end, but I do not think you understand the pressure his boss has been putting on him. We had a long talk about the project, and I think he now believes he can deliver the results you need. I suggest a more supportive relationship will help to achieve this.
> Regards
> Tim

A few hours later, he got this reply from Janine.

> Dear Tim
> I was shocked to hear from you. This is the first time during this particular project you have e-mailed me and it is to tell me how to do my job. Phil and I are working hard to turn round his side of the project, and I don't think your intervention will help. Certainly I have never been accused of not being supportive.
> Janine

Task Discuss these questions in groups.
   a What would you have done in this situation?
   b How could Tim have avoided this reaction from Janine?
   c What should Tim do now?

One person in each group should take notes on the discussion and give a short summary of the group's views.

E Language reference

Read through the key words and phrases below from this unit. Add any other useful words and expressions which you feel are important for you to learn. Make sure you find the time to review these words and phrases regularly and to use them at work.

Linking words
addition: in addition, furthermore, moreover
cause: therefore, consequently, due to
conclusion: in conclusion, finally, lastly
contrast: yet, however, whereas, despite, in spite of
generalisation: usually, normally, as a rule, in general, on the whole
reason: because, since, as, in response to

Key phrases for e-mails and letters
Beginnings
I am writing to request/enquire/inform/check/confirm/ask …
Just a quick e-mail to …
I am pleased/sorry to hear/learn that …
Endings
I look forward to meeting/seeing you next week / in January.
I am looking forward to seeing you / hearing from you.
Look forward to … / Looking forward to …
See you …
Requesting
I would be grateful if … / I would appreciate it if …
Could you send …?
Providing documentation
I am enclosing/attaching …
I enclose/attach …
Please find enclosed/attached …
Agreeing/Disagreeing
I agree / I cannot agree with/to …
I am happy to …
Unfortunately, I am unable to …
Making suggestions
I propose/suggest that …
I would (strongly) advise/recommend (that) …
It is advisable to …
Expressing urgency
at your earliest convenience
as soon as possible
without further delay
by Friday / the end of January
Apologising
I am sorry to hear/learn/see that …
I [do] apologise for … / Please accept our sincere apologies for …
Offering further assistance
Do not hesitate to contact us again if you require further assistance.
If you have any further questions, please contact me.
Please let me know if I can be of further assistance.

See page 89 for some e-mail templates to help you with your writing skills.

Writing task Choose two of the following writing activities. Integrate at least five standard expressions from above into the e-mails of your choice.
1 Write a reply to one of the two e-mails in Section D using a similar style.
2 Apologise to a colleague for not being able to attend his presentation yesterday and give a reason why. Ask him for a copy of his slides.
3 Request a catalogue from a new supplier you met two weeks ago at a trade fair in Frankfurt. Ask about possible discounts and product availability / delivery costs.
4 Thank your team for their contributions to the recent meeting. Invite them to suggest items for the next agenda. Circulate the minutes.

F Virtual working tips and personal action plan

1 **Take a few minutes to reflect on these tips for effective writing. Which do you think is the most important, and which ideas are most useful?**

> **TIP 1**
> Plan carefully before you write. Decide what your objective is, and what outcome you want from your message. Having a clear aim helps you to decide how long you need to spend on the task.
> Ideas for planning:
> - Make sure you have all the relevant information/documentation at hand. Be as precise as possible in your message and the action (if any) required by the recipient.
> - If the message is complex, note down the key points and check you include them all when you compose the e-mail. Read it back to yourself slowly and carefully and ask yourself 'Would I understand this if I received it? Would it make a good impression on me?'.

> **TIP 2**
> Be clear about the style of writing you choose.
> Ideas for style:
> - If you want to send the same message to a number of people at the same time, check your style and register (degree of formality you are using) to avoid using language which is acceptable to some but not all recipients.
> - Ask yourself if you require a response to your message. If so, make sure that is explicit. It is much better to write 'What do you think of the new format?' than 'I was wondering how people felt about the new format.'

> **TIP 3**
> Select the right language to convey the right style. Remember the acronym KISS (Keep It Short and Simple) and avoid using jargon or complex words where possible. Avoid repeating words and phrases. Start and end your writing with correct standard phrases. Pay careful attention to grammar, spelling and punctuation.
> Ideas for language use:
> - Review the format, style and language. You can often eliminate up to 50% of the grammar, punctuation and spelling mistakes you have made by taking time to check.
> - If you are still not confident about your written English, get feedback from a colleague before you press 'send'. People usually like being asked to help, and you will learn something from it, too.

2 **What other ideas for effective writing have you got from studying this unit?**

Personal action plan 3 **Think about what you have learned from this unit. Note down two or three important points which you want to apply to your own job (*What?*). Then create a schedule to implement your learning (*When?*) and think about the best way to check that you have successfully applied these ideas (*How?*).**

4 **Discuss your action plan and adapt it if necessary, based on any useful feedback you get.**

	what I learned and want to apply to my job	when/how I will apply this in my job	how I will check if I have applied it
1			
2			
3			

5 Effective writing

Building relationships

AIMS
A To analyse virtual relationships
B To develop effective virtual interpersonal skills
C To identify strategies for creating and sustaining trust
D To manage conflict caused by cultural differences

A Discussion and listening

Think about it

1 Which of these words and phrases concerning good working relationships are most important for you?

friendship   similar values   respect   a sense of humour
helpfulness   expertise   reliability   a similar working style

2 How can you develop good relationships when you meet new colleagues? What are the challenges if you don't have the chance to meet them face to face?

Listen to this

3 a 🎧 26 You are going to hear an interview with Ana Giménez, an expert on virtual team-building. She discusses the impact that good or bad relationships can have. Ana talks about her 'three-step model' for good relationships. Complete each of the three boxes below with *one* noun to identify each step.

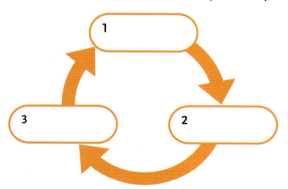

b 🎧 27 In the second part of the interview, Ana explains why emotions affect relationships negatively and positively. Listen, then complete this table with the qualities she mentions and the impact they can have on an employee's attitude.

effects	qualities	impact
negative	arrogance, lack of (a)	Subordinate feels they are not (b) .... Their (c) .... is reduced.
positive	warmth, (d) .... and (e)	They (f) .... well. They feel their contribution is (g) .... They feel (h) ....

4 What two extremes does Ana mention to show the impact of cultural background?

5 🎧 **28** Listen to the third part of the interview with Ana and answer these questions.

a Which three non-linguistic factors in communication does Ana mention?
b According to Ana, how should we 'manage' communication?
c What effect can silence have?
d Why are questions so important?

Focus on language **6** Ana talks about many personal factors connected to relationship-building. Look at the definitions below and match each one with a word from the box.

> attention   attitude   self-awareness   commitment
> curiosity   ~~rapport~~   respect

a a close and harmonious relationship in which the people or groups concerned understand each other's feelings or ideas and communicate well   *rapport*
b a feeling or opinion about something, especially when this shows in your behaviour
c a feeling of deep admiration for someone or something elicited by their abilities, qualities or achievements
d being willing to give your time and energy to something
e a strong desire to know or learn something
f watching, listening to or thinking about something or someone with interest
g concern about and interest in your own particular situation or development

7 Complete these sentences with the qualities from Exercise 6.

a We have a good ...*rapport*... because we are similar in temperament, we work well together and we like each other, too!
b How much .... we pay when people are talking about themselves is a very good indicator of how interested we are in them.
c She always wants to learn about what life is like in my country. She seems to have genuine .... towards our customs and values.
d He shows a lot of .... to the project, often working late, especially when we need to meet a deadline.
e I know I can sometimes be impatient when people don't respond immediately to my messages, and I hope this .... about my 'weakness' will help me to change!
f I have a lot of .... for his experience and the decisions he makes.
g She's always cheerful, and that positive .... to life makes me feel good too!

8 We often use expressions to talk about positive or negative attitudes in a relationship. Match these pairs of opposing attitudes.

1 What you see is what you get.
2 I admire her values.
3 She's very friendly.
4 She always appreciates my work. s
5 I always know I have her full attention.
6 I don't think she's good at her job.
7 I know she'll do it when she says she will.

a She never says 'thank you'.
b I respect her competence.
c I get the feeling she isn't listening.
d I never know if she'll do it until the last minute.
e I don't like her views on some issues.
f She's a bit cold and impersonal.
g It's hard to read her attitude.

Let's talk **9 a** In any relationship, it's good to 'start on the right foot'. Work with a partner, preferably back to back or online. Imagine that you do not know the other person. Try to discover things in common with them. Once you have finished your short conversation, move on to another person. Use the suggested conversation topics on page 90 to help you with the task.

b Compare the information you found in common. What kind of information about a person makes it easier for you to 'connect' with them?

6 Building relationships

B Communication skills: Effective virtual interpersonal skills

Think about it

1 How can you maintain your online relationships with colleagues? Which communication methods do you use, and why?

2 From your experience, how useful are social networking pages (like Facebook) for virtual relationships? What is your experience of using these applications?

Listen to this

3 🎧 **29–31** You are going to hear three people describing how they maintain online relationships with their colleagues.
- George: manager of a team working on strategic marketing planning based in Europe and Asia
- Angela: virtual project leader for a multinational global product development team
- Viola: project leader of a pan-European team working on a quality standards charter

Listen to each person and answer these questions.

🎧 **29** George
a What did George decide to do?
b Did all of his team like this idea?

🎧 **30** Angela
c Why did Angela use her own material as an example?
d Did everyone in her team produce similar material to hers?

🎧 **31** Viola
e Why doesn't Viola tell her team members when she will be calling?
f For Viola, what is it very important to remember?

4 🎧 **29–31** Listen to all three people again and decide whether these sentences are true (T) or false (F).
a Some people didn't like George's idea.
b George thinks we wouldn't see each other as 'human' without the social element.
c Angela expected everyone to use her model for their presentations.
d Angela is not totally certain everyone liked her idea.
e Viola prefers fixed times for informal phone conversations.
f Viola doesn't share her personal worries with her team members.

5 Which of the three ideas do you most like – George's, Angela's or Viola's? Why?

Focus on language

6 a When establishing closer relationships, native speakers often like to use idiomatic phrases to express feelings and attitudes. The idioms in bold in the sentences below all refer to communication. Complete each of the sentences with a word from the box.

| ~~line~~ | mind | nutshell | straight | wavelength | wrong |

a Hi, Tomas. I suppose you're busy ... I'm sorry if it's a bad moment to talk. Shall I **drop you a** _line_ later?
b I phoned Johanssen from Swedbank. Good news. Sounds like we are **on the same** _____ regarding the joint venture!
c I'd like it if you could give me positive *and* negative feedback. Feel free to **speak your** _____ if you aren't happy with my proposal.
d Thanks for the question, Helga. Yes, I did work with Bob Anderson and, **to put it in a** _____ , it was a 'complicated' relationship.
e That isn't what I meant to say – please don't **get the** _____ **end of the stick!**
f Good to hear your voice! I'll **get** _____ **to the point**. We need you to prepare the testing data for a presentation. Can you do that?

60   6 Building relationships

b Now match each of the idioms in Exercise 6a with one of these definitions.
   a contact someone in writing *drop someone a line*
   b a brief summary
   c speak directly and briefly
   d with similar ideas and opinions
   e express an opinion sincerely
   f misunderstand/misinterpret a message

7 These sentences are further examples of how you can express attitude. Match each sentence (1–7) with its more idiomatic equivalent in bold (a–g).
   1 I want to make a suggestion which some of you won't like.
   2 With a bit of luck, we'll get approval for the budget.
   3 I'm uncertain about what decision to make.
   4 To be honest, I have a fundamentally bad feeling about what's happening.
   5 I wish I hadn't made such a quick decision.
   6 Can you tell us if you agree or not?
   7 I have both a positive and a negative attitude to this idea.

   a I'm **in two minds** about the new position. It has positive and negative aspects.
   b I'm **keeping my fingers crossed** that the new budget will be approved.
   c I suppose, **deep down**, I'm not satisfied with the situation.
   d I'm **having second thoughts** about agreeing to lead this project. It's a disaster!
   e I'm **playing devil's advocate** here, but can't we do this without telling the steering committee?
   f I **have mixed feelings** about him – his ideas are great, but he's so unreliable.
   g You can't **sit on the fence** forever! Are you against or in favour?

Let's talk **8 Emoticons and abbreviations can save time when you want to express attitude or emotion in instant messaging or e-mails. What do the ones shown below mean to you? In which situations would you use them? Discuss with a partner and compare your views.**

   a graphic emoticons

      1   2   3   4   5   6

   b abbreviations
      1 OMG!   2 fyi   3 tyvm   4 asap   5 cu l8r?
   c text emoticons
      1 XD   2 :-P   3 >:(

9 Do you think all five of the abbreviations in Exercise 8b are appropriate for use in written business communication? Why? / Why not?

'Gee, Bill, you're not still upset about that e-mail I sent you yesterday, are you?'

6 Building relationships

C Professional skills: Creating and sustaining trust

Think about it

> Love all, trust a few, do wrong to none.
>
> William Shakespeare (1564–1616), English dramatist

> Men trust their ears less than their eyes.
>
> Herodotus (484–425 BC), ancient Greek historian, 'the father of history'

1 Read the two quotations above and discuss these questions.
   a What does each quotation say to you?
   b Which do you agree with more?
   c How can you create trust when you work virtually?

Read this

2 Read the text below and answer these questions.
   a What is the purpose of the examples of the trapeze artists and the dentist?
   b Why is it not a good idea to use extended eye contact as an indicator of trust?
   c What characteristics should a virtual team leader search for to help establish trust?
   d What is necessary to create a 'systematic approach'?

How we determine trust

Trapeze artists trust each other not to lose their grip. It is literally a matter of life and death. When we go to our dentist, we trust them to have (a) the competence to diagnose and treat any problems we might have, and (b) the motor skills and sensitivity of touch not to cause us unbearable pain when they are exploring inside our mouths!

Obviously, the two examples above are fairly extreme, but they do demonstrate the importance of this fundamental feeling we need to develop towards people who have, in some way or other, our well-being, peace of mind and, in some cases, even our professional future in their hands.

When we want to evaluate the degree of trust we can place in a particular person, there is usually some demonstrable way of measuring this. It can be based on the way people behave or speak (or don't speak), which is observable. Western Europeans, for example, may hesitate before trusting someone who doesn't look them in the eyes when speaking directly to them, as that body language is seen as a sign of potential untrustworthiness. If they are dealing with a South-East Asian colleague, they need to be aware that this body language needs to be read and interpreted in a completely different way. The point is, though, that what we see and hear combined can inform us about how much we can trust someone. In a virtual context, that element is minimised, even if you have access to a good video-conferencing platform.

The findings of recent research indicate that cultural factors in the way people communicate are important in building and maintaining trust. Examples include frequency of contact, length of occasions when that contact takes place and having a specific set of actions in place to welcome a new team member on board and make sure they start operating from the very beginning with a sense of shared values and common ways of behaving. The informed choice of communication channels and an awareness of a person's local context greatly encourage a rapid sense of competence and inclusion. Therefore, trust in a global virtual team requires some preliminary thought and engagement with the team to establish a virtual environment that makes the most sense.

Done wisely, with sufficient time and consultation with team members, this virtual team is much more likely to develop actions that encourage good use of its collective culture, which in turn will lead to greater overall effectiveness of performance.

With regard to communication, successful virtual teams will have a systematic approach where people can be heard and understood and where predictability (within reason), availability and mutual responsiveness and responsibility will become norms which will greatly help trust to be the foundation of all the team's activities.

adapted from Mockaitis, A., Rose, E. and Zettinig, P. *The determinants of trust in multicultural global virtual teams*. Academy of Management Annual Meeting Proceedings, 2009

3 There are several references to the qualities required for virtual trust in the text. Find words or expressions which mean the following:
   a able to be seen/noted
   b understood (an action, mood or behaviour) as having a particular meaning
   c displaying, or based on, reliable information
   d give support, confidence or hope to (someone)
   e reacting quickly and positively towards each other's suggestions, ideas or efforts (*two words*)

4 Think of a person you trust completely (e.g. a colleague). What qualities do they have? Use words from the text and Exercise 3 to help you. Describe this person to a partner.

Focus on language

5 One model for trust identifies ten factors. Match each quality (1–10) with its definition (a–j).

1 competence
2 openness
3 integrity
4 reciprocity
5 compatability
6 goodwill
7 predictability
8 well-being
9 inclusion
10 accessibility

a being available and approachable to offer advice and/or support
b showing empathy, support and strong care and commitment towards others
c being reliable and consistent; doing what you promise to do
d showing initial trust in others so that they will show trust in you
e involving and engaging everyone to enhance and increase commitment
f having ethical principles that guide your behaviour
g being good at your job
h communicating common values, interests and experiences
i being happy to share knowledge and information
j returning favours to people who do favours for you

6 a These five sentences all contain idiomatic expressions referring to one or more of the qualities in Exercise 5. Match each sentence (a–e) with its corresponding quality (1–10).

a Wen Li and I **get on like a house on fire**. We spend hours outside work time on Messenger talking about **everything under the sun** – work or otherwise.
b I like her, because, in terms of character, **what you see is what you get**, and she is **as regular as clockwork** when it comes to reporting back.
c She's been a valuable team member because she's really competent and **knows** this project **like the back of her hand**.
d I value the fact that she doesn't try to hide things from us – good, bad or indifferent news, she always **lays her cards on the table** and would never try to **be economical with the truth**.
e Olaf has always had **an open-door policy** as a team leader, so if we need to **get something off our chests**, we know who to call or text.

b What do you think each expression in bold means?

Let's talk

7 Share with a partner some of your own experiences of virtual relationships. What qualities (positive or negative) were significant? What made them good or bad?

8 a There are many people we interact with, either via spoken or written communication, whom we never see. Choose some of the examples in the box and discuss how these people can develop a sense of trust purely on the basis of non-face-to-face contact.

a radio news journalist ⟷	a regular listener
a responder in a call centre ⟷	a consumer
a helpline operator at a bank ⟷	a bank customer
a health hotline responder ⟷	an ill person
an online retailer ⟷	an online customer
an online language trainer ⟷	an online language learner

b What other virtual relationships do you have? How easy is it to develop trust without seeing/meeting the other person?

6 Building relationships

D Intercultural competence: Managing conflict caused by cultural differences

1 What could cause intercultural conflict among colleagues working virtually? What are the best ways to deal with this? Discuss with a partner.

2 Read the text below about responses to conflict from different cultural perspectives, then answer these questions.

   a What are the typical differences in attitude between 'individualists' and 'collectivists' in situations of conflict?

   b How can the way we are socialised affect our response to conflict?

   c How can the way we use our voice affect another person?

Comfort with conflict

Individualists and collectivists view conflict differently. Collectivists, who place a high value on harmony, see conflict as a sign of social failure. As a result, comfort levels with conflict situations, especially of an interpersonal nature, are low. While many individualists also feel discomfort with conflict, it is acknowledged as an inevitable part of life that must be dealt with. However, being in conflict with someone is not necessarily something to be ashamed about.

Communication styles

There are a number of factors that contribute to communication style. One factor is the extent to which one is expressive or restrained. Some team members may have been socialised to reveal strong emotions. Others may be more indirect, covering their emotions behind a 'poker face', using monotone speech and avoiding eye contact.

These different communication styles are not problematic in themselves. However, problems can arise, for example, if team members disagree and one person represents their views and feelings forcefully with a raised voice. Another more restrained team member may see that as arrogant. The same 'arrogant' team member may conclude that the restrained team member is untrustworthy because the message they are receiving is not clear and explicit.

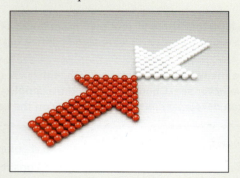

Another area of difference relates to directness. Some cultures are very direct. They like to get straight to the point, and get frustrated with someone who 'beats around the bush'. Indirect cultures prefer to deal with relational aspects first, and to restore harmony before addressing substantive issues.

adapted from www.mediate.com

3 Do you think it is better to deal with conflict openly or try to maintain harmony? Discuss and compare your views in small groups.

4 Work in pairs. You are going to resolve two situations of potential conflict.
Student A: Turn to page 90.
Student B: Turn to page 92.

Case study: The international quality standards team

Background Michael Cleber works as Production Support Manager for Hanstock Pharma, a German pharmaceuticals company which supplies ingredients to manufacturers. Two years ago, his company took over Genuschem, a North American company. Genuschem has three production plants in the US, supplying the US and Latin American markets. After the takeover, a global team was set up to share best practice and develop a worldwide strategy for quality control. The team is made up of three Americans, one German, one Swiss and one Singaporean. Their contact is 90% virtual, with an annual 'get together' in California to attend workshops and networking events. This yearly event is closely organised and seen by the company as a chance to network and enhance relationships among global colleagues.

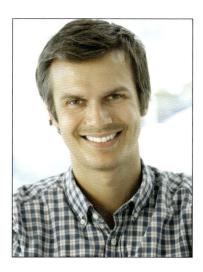

Situation For some time, Michael has felt frustrated about the lack of harmonious relationships in the team. Christopher Morris (US) has assumed the role of team leader without any formal decision being made. Eric Prinz (US) is Production Support Manager at the biggest plant in the US, but is a most reluctant participant in meetings, often giving the impression he would prefer to be somewhere else.

Kim Lee (Singaporean) never attends, and Michael would like to know why. Bob Armstrong (US) is the oldest member, two years away from retirement. He has emerged as the 'father' of the group and is the person Michael feels closest to personally. Marie Würtz (Swiss) doesn't say very much, but clearly dislikes Eric's attitude during meetings and sometimes makes indirect comments indicating this. Thomas Hassler (German) is Michael's counterpart at the second plant in Germany. He is much less experienced than Michael and appears to see himself in the junior role at the German end.

Tasks

1. 🎧 32 Michael is beginning to question how useful the weekly team meetings are. Listen to a short extract from a phone conversation he has with Marie after a recent conference call. Take notes on what they talk about.

2. Discuss these questions.
   a Why could this situation create conflict?
   b If you were Michael, how would you deal with this situation?

3. Imagine you are planning the agenda for the next San Francisco conference. The list below gives some suggestions and possible issues to consider. Add to it and discuss possible activities with the group. Choose the best ideas.

- 'Get it out into the open' session (airing problems)? Dangerous?
- Outdoor 'action' team-building day?
- Social events to promote closer personal bonding? What?
- Creation of a group Facebook page and Twitter account?
- Group creation of 'Dos and Don'ts' for future communication?

6 Building relationships

E Language reference

Read through the key words and phrases below from this unit. Add any other useful words and expressions which you feel are important for you to learn. Make sure you find the time to review these words and phrases regularly and to use them at work.

Positive and negative personality traits

Positive	Negative
modest/humble	arrogant
warm	cold/distant
friendly	unfriendly
helpful	unhelpful
trustworthy	untrustworthy
reliable	unreliable
inclusive	exclusive
accessible	remote/distant
proactive	reactive / lacking initiative
competent	incompetent

to be (in)compatible with someone
to show/demonstrate goodwill towards someone
a(n) good/positive/open/helpful attitude
a(n) bad/unhealthy/suspicious/unhelpful approach

Relationship-building verbs/actions
be aware of (differences / personality / communication style)
show commitment (to) / be committed to
show/demonstrate interest (in)
be interested in
pay attention to (someone/something)
do someone a favour
congratulate someone (on doing something)

Showing interest and curiosity in others
Where exactly are you from?
Is it a big place?
Really?
That's interesting ... tell me more!
What's your background?
Did you train as a (chemist)?
Why did you (change career)?

Things in common
I met a colleague of yours ...
We work in that sector as well.
Do you know Hans Becker? I worked with him in ...

Interests
What do you do when you aren't working?
Really? How long have you been (–ing)?
That must be challenging!

Asking about experience
What (exactly) do you do?
How long have you been (doing that)?
What do you like about it?
Have you always worked there?
How do you feel about (using social media / running a virtual team / conference-calling)?

Writing task Choose one of the following writing tasks. Integrate at least five standard expressions from above into your e-mail.
1 Write an e-mail introducing yourself at the beginning of a virtual project. This will be your virtual 'business card', so think carefully about the image you want to give.
2 Write a personal profile for your 'My Page' of the internal social-media platform used in your organisation.

F Virtual working tips and personal action plan

1 **Take a few minutes to reflect on these tips for relationship-building. Which do you think is the most important, and which ideas are most useful?**

TIP 1

Be proactive. Many people think that virtual communication is the same as face-to-face communication, but you need to compensate for lack of visibility by using language much more than normal. This means taking the initiative: ask questions, use people's names, ask for clarification, clarify and summarise frequently.
Ideas for being proactive:
- Avoid long silences in conference calls. Ask questions, express your views. Silence is ambiguous, and you need to know its causes. Are people thinking? confused? angry?
- If no one is involving you in the call, an effective way to interrupt is to use the name of the person talking. They will usually stop, and you can then politely intervene.

TIP 2

Build and maintain relationships. Finding five minutes to make a quick call to a colleague on the other side of the world can help their morale tremendously. Investing time at the beginning of the relationship creates and cements connections between two individuals who may never meet face to face.
Ideas for building relationships:
- If you are the facilitator, log in to a conference call a little early and welcome the others as they join the call.
- You could also identify the quieter participants and give them a phone call either before or after the meeting/call, just to give them the opportunity to express any problems they may be having.

TIP 3

Model the type of behaviour you want from your colleagues, as it is more likely they will copy that behaviour. Be courteous, open-minded and, above all, interested. By being self-aware, you will know more about the impact of your communication style on other people.
Ideas for modelling good behaviour:
- Make a note on your desk to remember to do this. Sometimes, when you are tired or unenthusiastic, your behaviour can reflect this. Write a short list of the qualities you want to exhibit and check them off as you actually perform them.
- Take a little time to discover what makes you tick. Knowing about yourself and your impact on other people helps you to exploit your strengths and minimise your weaknesses.

Personal action plan 2 **Think about what you have learned from this unit. Note down two or three important points which you want to apply to your own job (*What?*). Then create a schedule to implement your learning (*When?*) and think about the best way to check that you have successfully applied these ideas (*How?*).**

3 **Discuss your action plan and adapt it if necessary, based on any useful feedback you get.**

	what I learned and want to apply to my job	when/how I will apply this in my job	how I will check if I have applied it
1			
2			
3			

7 Managing diversity

AIMS

A To examine what influences diversity
B To consider how to adapt communication styles
C To learn to use diversity for effective collaboration
D To become aware of cultural diversity

A Discussion and listening

Think about it

> Variety is the spice of life.
> Traditional proverb

> We need diversity of thought in the world to face the new challenges.
> Tim Berners-Lee (1955–), British physicist (the inventor of the Web)

1 Look at the two quotations above. Is variety the same as diversity? Do you agree with Tim Berners-Lee that 'diversity of thought' can help us?

2 Which aspects of diversity listed in the box are most significant for you in the workplace? What other examples of diversity can you think of?

> age   gender   attitude to technology   nationality
> region   religion   job   job function
> communication style   personality   working style

3 Which aspects of diversity could have a particular impact on people working virtually? Which have had an impact on you?

Listen to this

4 🎧 **33** You are going to hear two virtual team members, Nils Lindstrom from Norway and Heather Rawson from Scotland, talking about how diversity has an impact on group dynamics. Listen and answer these questions.
  a Which three locations does Nils give as examples of diversity?
  b What examples does Heather give to show how mistaken ideas can have an effect on the way we see people?
  c What is extremely important for Nils when working with diverse groups? Why?

5 a 🎧 **34** Heather and Nils go on to talk about what factors to take into account when working with diverse groups of people. Listen and complete this table.

Factor 1: Planning **(a)**	Some like **(b)** .... planning, others prefer a more **(c)** .... approach.
Factor 2: Guidelines for dealing with **(d)**	Get the **(e)** .... out into the open.
Factor 3: **(f)** .... the situation before it gets **(g)**	Some people are indirect and others are **(h)** .... Some personalities are outgoing and others are **(i)** ....

  b What does Nils suggest as the other two factors?

68   7 Managing diversity

6 In your opinion, which of the key factors mentioned in Exercise 5 is easiest to address? Which is the most difficult?

Focus on language **7** This diagram illustrates four areas of potential diversity in communication and working styles when working virtually. Complete the diversity factors connected to each key area using the words and phrases in the box below.

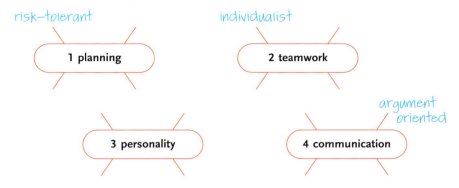

implicit and indirect   structured and rigid   dependent   ~~risk-tolerant~~
explicit and direct   organic and adaptable   collectivist   flexible roles
autonomous   risk-averse   ~~individualist~~   consensus-oriented   defined roles
~~argument-oriented~~   personable and talkative   cautious and quiet

8 Complete each of these sentences with words and phrases from Exercise 7.
   a We don't really have a common way of dealing with items on the agenda, so everyone just contributes. Our approach to conference-calling is .... and .... , rather than .... and ....
   b I would say that he's quite .... and .... as a person, because he doesn't say much and he never really sounds confident. She's completely different, much more .... and .... – not only does she explain her decisions at length, but she also makes you feel good about her message!
   c Patrick is very .... and .... in the way he presents ideas. You know exactly what he wants, even if it sounds a bit rude at times! Janina, on the other hand, is much more .... and .... You need to 'read between the lines'.
   d In the last team I was a member of, the dynamic was very .... – basically, it was 'every man/woman for him/herself'. My present team is much more .... in its principles. We all share in our successes and we all take responsibility for our failures.

Let's talk **9** Your virtual team leader has sent you a series of guidelines for team communication. You think there is too much information there and that the document is poorly presented. Discuss which guidelines can be omitted and which are essential for establishing efficient communication. Would you establish rules like these in your virtual communication environment? Why? / Why not?

> Only e-mail communication.
> Meetings last no longer than one hour.
> Calls always at 12:00 CET.
> Agenda not fixed – decided at start of call.
> All team members have to attend all calls/meetings.
> Team leader always acts as facilitator and minute-taker.
> Precise (verbatim) minutes only.
> All instant-message communication to be recorded and stored.
> Participants must find a quiet place to take call.
> Minute-taker can use any format for minutes.
> Briefing documents and agenda must be distributed at least 48 hours before call.

B Communication skills: Adapting communication styles

Think about it

1 How far are you prepared to be flexible and adapt to using different communication channels or styles when working with colleagues from different backgrounds?

2 How far do you think others should adapt to your style?

Listen to this

3 a You are going to listen to three international colleagues talking about themselves, their jobs and their communication styles.
- **Rajat** (India) is a human resources manager working with a team of 30 people.
- **Henning** (Norway) is a laboratory manager and team member on an international project.
- **Isabel** (Argentina) is leader of a global trouble-shooting team present in several markets.

This table shows their preferred channels of communication. Before you listen, briefly consider why each person might feel the way they do about the different communication methods.

	phone	e-mail	documentation	conference call	IM
Rajat	✓			✗	
Henning		✓	✓	✗	✓
Isabel			✗	✓	

b 🎧 35–37 Listen and check to see if your predictions were correct.

4 🎧 38–40 Listen to short extracts from the three speakers in Exercise 3. How does each person think they can improve their virtual communication skills?
a Rajat thinks he needs to …
b Henning wants to be better at …
c Isabel needs to spend more time …

5 a What are the most common ways of communicating virtually in your organisation? Look at this table and add information about specific tasks and activities connected to them in each column. Some examples have been given for you.

tasks	people and relationships
• Making minutes available – on the intranet	• Planning a meeting – by instant messaging • Asking for a favour – by phone

b Now tell your partner about the items on your list and ask each other these questions.
   a Is this the best way of communicating?
   b Do you need to improve any specific areas of your communication?

Focus on language

6 Match each term (1–6) with its definition (a–f).

1 a suggestion
2 gratitude
3 a reminder
4 an enquiry
5 a request
6 praise

a The act of asking politely or formally for something
b The act of asking for information
c A proposition for a line of action, for a group or for a speaker
d A demonstration of appreciation for an act of kindness
e An expression of warm approval or admiration
f An action that causes someone to remember something

> **Tip**
> People can communicate in very different ways. For example, if someone says, 'When you have a minute, can you forward that file to me?', they are making a request, saying 'I want you to do something for me.'

7 Match each of these examples (a–j) with one of the terms from Exercise 6 (1–6). There is one term that is not used.

a I'm very impressed with what you've produced.
b Forward me that e-mail from Jean-Luc as soon as possible!
c I suggest we hold meetings once every two weeks. What do you think?
d Would you mind getting in touch with Arja?
e Don't forget to call Pau before the telco, will you?
f Cheers.
g Nice work.
h I really appreciate your help.
i Let's merge the two documents to create a master copy.
j Please make sure you remember to attach the right version of the report.

8 With a partner, take it in turns to say each of the examples in Exercise 7. Your partner listens and provides the answer. Then discuss the response.

Let's talk

9 Work in groups of four. Read this background information.

You are going to have a conference call with colleagues to give feedback on a new energy soft drink aimed at the sports and leisure market. This product was recently launched as a limited trial in four key markets. If consumer response from this trial is positive, the product will be launched in these markets in the next six months. Senior management then want a unified marketing strategy for a global launch. They want production to be concentrated in two large plants (for reasons of economies of scale).
The aim of the conference call is to:
- get feedback from each of the market managers on the consumer response to the trial launch;
- discuss, evaluate and decide on the options available for action (based on the feedback).

Student A: Turn to page 89.
Student B: Turn to page 91.
Student C: Turn to page 93.
Student D: Turn to page 94.

10 Using the feedback table on page 91, give feedback to each other on how well you all performed.

7 Managing diversity

C Professional skills: Using diversity for effective collaboration

Think about it

1 Think about your experiences of being a member of a team (work and non-work). Which were the best experiences? Why?

2 What factors create a sense of 'team spirit'? Do the same factors apply to virtual teams?

Read this

3 Read the text below, then answer these questions.
  a Why do groups with more variety of cognitive diversity often do better than groups with one way of working?
  b Why can cultural diversity encourage creativity and effectiveness?
  c What is necessary for preference diversity to work effectively?

Three forms of diversity

We often assume that we'll get better results from groups of people from different backgrounds and possessing a variety of skills than we would from groups with a single orientation. That means diversity of many types, not only differences of culture, ethnicity and gender, but also variety of expertise, intellectual perspective, values and interests. They are all important for collaborative groups.

Cognitive diversity
All forms of diversity are not equally effective. It's the differences in perspectives and methods of approaching problems that most often lead to better outcomes. This is what is called 'cognitive diversity'. Differing ways of looking at the world, interpreting experience, solving problems and predicting future possibilities work together to produce a distinctive mental tool set. Groups with this sort of variety consistently outperform groups working with a single problem-solving perspective.

Identity diversity
When it comes to collaborative groups, diversity usually refers to cultural, ethnic and gender balance. Identity diversity satisfies the need for fairness and equality, but, by itself, doesn't guarantee better problem-solving. The evidence of various studies indicates that cultural diversity has the most significant impact.
  The variety of cultural and ethnic backgrounds often correlates with more creative and effective solutions because differing cultural perspectives, language and experience can also mean different ways of thinking about and defining problems.

Preference diversity
Probably the first thing that comes to mind in putting together a collaborative group is to include the full range of interest groups most likely to be affected by a decision – and most likely to oppose it if they are excluded. Isn't diversity of interests essential to coming up with a better solution than one devised by a group representing a single interest?
  In fact, the most consistently disruptive element that emerges from research is divergence of interests and values – or preference diversity. Drawn into a collaborative group, they are often not communicating well but still battling over fixed positions. If such groups can find a way to establish an effective working relationship, they are likely to be extremely good at producing creative solutions. But if they cannot get on, they can fail pretty badly.

adapted from a blog by John Folk Williams, an expert in cross-cultural collaboration

Focus on language

4 Match each of the words in bold in the expressions on the left (1–5) with its definition (a–e).

1 **nature** of communication
2 conflicting **priorities**
3 **disruptive** element
4 **underlying** attitudes
5 cultural **perspectives**

a a thing/task regarded as more important than others
b present but not obvious; implicit
c a particular attitude to or way of regarding something
d characterised by unrest or disorder
e type, kind

5 Use the expressions relating to diversity from Exercise 4 to complete these sentences.

a Although they seem to work well together on the surface, there are .... that could create problems later.
b He's a .... when we are discussing issues because he is constantly interrupting.
c Regarding what is polite or not, the .... of northern Europeans are significantly different to those of, say, countries in the Arab world.
d His unwillingness to attend conference calls has an obvious effect on the .... of our ....
e If we can't resolve the .... between your obligations to the local team and our international project, I'll have to find another person to take over.

6 Where there are differences of opinion between colleagues, it can be very helpful to restate those differences in a less direct way. Look at these four strategies for doing this, then rewrite the sentences below using one or more of these strategies.

- Use *not* with a positive word instead of the obvious negative (e.g. *not very convenient*):
  It's going to be really difficult. → *It **isn't** going to be very **easy**.*
- Use *would, could* or *might* to make language less dogmatic:
  This is a problem. → *This **might** be a problem.*
- Use questions. Present your needs as requests not demands, and use negative questions to make suggestions more open:
  We should do it now. → ***Wouldn't** it be better to do it now?*
- Use qualifying or restricting words to 'soften' your message:
  That's impossible. → *(**I'm afraid**) that's **very** / **quite** / **a bit** / **a little** / **rather** / **slightly** hard.*

a That's a stupid suggestion!
b The conference call will have to be in the afternoon.
c That is unacceptable.
d I'm too busy to do it now.
e That report he wrote was terrible!

Let's talk

7 Discuss with a partner the possible advantages and disadvantages of team diversity in these cases. Take opposing positions for each subject in order to practise expressing diverse opinions. Try to persuade your partner to agree with you.

- being very time-conscious *vs* being flexible about time
- a face-to-face meeting *vs* a conference call
- preferring written communication *vs* preferring spoken communication
- limiting technology use to work hours *vs* using technology in your personal life
- multi-tasking *vs* doing one task at a time
- avoiding personal use of social media *vs* embracing social-media networks

D Intercultural competence: Awareness of cultural diversity

1 Discuss these questions with a partner.
   a If it's 10:00 in Berlin, what time is it in São Paulo, Sydney and Tokyo?
   b How many time zones do you usually operate in?
   c In your virtual meetings, is there ever a mixture of native and non-native English speakers? What factors do you need to consider?

2 Read the text below and answer these questions.
   a Why is it important to consider the time you arrange a conference call or meeting?
   b How can we improve the experience for non-native speakers in conference calls?
   c Why is it sometimes useful for people to write during conference calls?
   d What effect can the time of day have on performance in virtual communication?

Why time zones and language matter to international teams

Time zones and language differences are among the important reasons virtual teams fail. Here are four things managers of international teams should consider if they want to keep their team cohesive and engaged:

1 **Galileo was right – you're not the centre of the universe.** When you're based at headquarters, it's very easy to presume that everyone works the same schedule you do. The fact is, breakfast in San Francisco is tea time in London, late evening in Bangalore and who knows what time tomorrow in Auckland. Most people will adjust to accommodate the boss's schedule, but it's the expectation that they *always* should that makes them crazy. Would it kill you to share the pain a bit? You'd be surprised how much goodwill you get in return.

2 **Everyone speaks English, so what's the problem?** Just because everyone on your team is able to function in a common language doesn't mean they do their best work that way. Employees functioning in foreign languages often aren't comfortable interrupting or making extensive points in conference calls. They may need time to clarify details before they're ready to give quality feedback. Build time for reflection into decision-making or you might miss the benefit of some very good thinking.

3 **There's no 'spell check' for accents.** Many foreign employees feel at a disadvantage because they aren't as persuasive verbally as they are in writing. While it's important to manage time, not every decision needs to be made immediately. Give people space to formulate a response and allow for healthy written discussion and questions, even via instant messaging during the call.

4 **How clear is *your* thinking at five in the morning?** We all know our own body clock. Are you a morning person? If so, you probably schedule important discussions for the morning, otherwise you'll be tired and irritable. Why would your virtual teammates be different? On just a pure productivity basis, apart from the human one, shouldn't you consider the role that time and working conditions play?

adapted from an article by Wayne Turmell
(author and blogger on effective virtual communication)

3 Look at these e-mail excerpts written by two people working virtually, sent to colleagues outside their team. Each one expresses frustration at a problem.

> When I listen back to recordings of our conference calls, I always sound a bit quiet, as if I wasn't sure of myself. I get interrupted a lot, too. I want to be able to contribute to the level of my professional expertise, but I never have enough thinking time to do so.

> The native speakers in our international management team speak far too fast for me to take in what they're saying. They also use a lot of colloquial language among themselves, making it even harder to follow.

Have you experienced similar problems? Explain your own experiences to your partner or group.

Case study: Crossed wires

Background Mireia works for a multinational clothing company. For the last six months, she has been a member of a global team responsible for unifying payroll software worldwide. The overall aim of the project is to standardise procedures so that all data can easily be transferred between backroom offices on different continents. At present, each operating centre uses its own payroll system. There are 15 members spread across five continents and nine markets, so the scope of the project is ambitious. Anthony, a British IT specialist, has been the project leader for the last 14 months. He has a lot of experience on this type of large-scale project and has led multinational teams before.

Situation Mireia thinks Anthony is a good project leader. He has good leadership qualities, he motivates everyone, he gives members a good degree of responsibility and control over their particular areas of activity, and he keeps the team on track and focused. However, Mireia is worried about his approach to leading the team's regular conference calls. His wide experience of team leadership often means he is rather impatient with less-experienced and younger colleagues, and he has a reputation for being very direct and abrasive at times.

The situation has reached the stage where Mireia is beginning to ask herself if she still wants to work on this team in the longer term. She is getting the feeling her ideas are not being listened to or valued.

Tasks 1 Mireia is thinking about the problem. What are the main issues in this case? Take notes on these areas:
- Anthony's style of conference-call facilitation
- The Latin American team members
- Conflicting approaches to communication of ideas
- The Dutch, German and Russian team members

2 How could Mireia address her problems with her line manager?

> I don't find Anthony an easy person to communicate with. We have a conference call once a week where we update each other on activities, and he has a very particular way of managing these calls – he interrupts if he feels someone's been talking for too long and he imposes a strict time limit, which wasn't agreed originally. There are four of us who are from the three Latin American markets. When we need to express ideas or opinions, Anthony is extremely directive, and some of us find this approach too limiting. Our way of communicating is to express ideas and opinions by building on previous contributions. This can be valuable, because the sum is often greater than the individual parts, and this is how we like to work in the Lat-Am markets. Anthony's approach is very structured. He seems to think we can all produce our ideas in a 'pre-packaged' way, but I don't work like that. We have other members of the team – Dutch, German, Russian – who don't seem to have this problem. Their approach to communication is very logical and rational, and they make their points in a very structured way. Anthony almost seems to show preference for this way of communicating during the calls. I always leave feeling frustrated and irritated. Not having face-to-face contact also complicates the situation, because I'm sure he would appreciate my point of view much more if we could have a chat about it over a coffee. I'm even beginning to ask myself if I still want to work on this team in the longer term. I'm getting the feeling my ideas are not being listened to.

7 Managing diversity

E Language reference

Read through the key words and phrases below from this unit. Add any other useful words and expressions which you feel are important for you to learn. Make sure you find the time to review these words and phrases regularly and to use them at work.

Cross-cultural diversity

task-oriented person	relationship-oriented person
time-flexible activities	time-restricted activities
hierarchical organisation	flat organisation
risk-tolerant approach	risk-averse approach
organic planning	structured planning

Diversity factors
age (young, old, middle-aged)
gender (male, female)
location (time zones, technology infrastructure, bandwidth)
communication style (direct, indirect, short, long, complex, simple, etc.)
status (senior management, middle-management, technical personnel, project leader)
functional area (business: marketing, sales, strategy, HR; technical: R&D, production)
personality (extrovert, introvert, quiet, loud, listener, speaker)
language used (competence: high, low, extensive, limited)

Functional language
Suggesting
Let's …
How about –*ing*?
Why don't we …?
Shall we …?
I suggest (that) we …
I think we should …
Requesting/demanding/ordering
Send me … (will you?)
I want you to send me …
Will you send me … , (please)?
Can you send me … , please?
Would you mind sending me …?
I'd appreciate it if you could send me …
I'd be (very) grateful if you could send me …
Praising
Well done!
Thanks a lot for –*ing* …
I'm very impressed with what you have achieved.
I appreciate all the work you've done.

Writing task Do one or both of the following writing activities. Integrate at least five standard expressions from above into your e-mail(s).
1 Write a reply to Mireia (Section D, Case study), sympathising with her situation and advising her on how she can improve things with Anthony.
2 Imagine you are creating a virtual team which will be working in your area of speciality. Write an advertisement of no more than 150 words, which will then be posted on the company's intranet for internal employees to apply.

F Virtual working tips and personal action plan

1 **Take a few minutes to reflect on these tips for relationship-building. Which do you think is the most important, and which ideas are most useful?**

TIP 1

Standardise as far as possible. A frequent complaint from virtual employees is that the leader doesn't lead. As a leader, the time you spend establishing norms (at or near the beginning of the process) is an investment in the future. Firstly, efficiency and respecting deadlines. Secondly, the degree of collaboration, information-sharing and expertise that occurs if people have clear procedures at the start of a process.
Ideas for standardising teamwork:
- Discuss and agree with the group on common ways to proceed before the work situation starts (if possible). This can involve contacting people individually or as a group, and asking them to provide norms and rules.
- Highlight and celebrate activities where success is achieved through collaboration and using the set of rules in a harmonious way.

TIP 2

Gain awareness through research and active listening. Explore differences, discuss them openly and try to reach compromise on an acceptable solution. Where there is an opportunity to speak one-to-one, do so, as it creates more enduring trust.
Idea for exploring differences:
- Many experienced virtual communicators comment that it is often the interactions they have in 'downtime' (for example, chatting at the beginning of a conference call) that can be extremely useful in the long run. Try doing this when you have the opportunity, to learn more about your colleagues' thoughts and perceptions.

TIP 3

Be prepared to adapt your own style of communication. If you are task-oriented, be aware that other colleagues may not be, so be flexible towards each other's approach. The approach of 'That's how I am, and I can't (and won't) change!' may not be successful in the long run, even if it brings short-term compliance.
Ideas for adapting your communication style:
- Try doing things differently from normal. If you speak a lot, speak less at today's conference call. Listen a lot. Ask more questions than usual. If you are generally quiet, intervene more.
- We spend a lot of time in our comfort zones when communicating. Be conscious of this and try to take more risks. This may mean making more mistakes, or not being as fluent as normal, but there are potential benefits. Listen to yourself later to assess your impact.

Personal action plan 2 **Think about what you have learned from this unit. Note down two or three important points which you want to apply to your own job (*What?*). Then create a schedule to implement your learning (*When?*) and think about the best way to check that you have successfully applied these ideas (*How?*).**

3 **Discuss your action plan and adapt it if necessary, based on any useful feedback you get.**

	what I learned and want to apply to my job	when/how I will apply this in my job	how I will check if I have applied it
1			
2			
3			

Teams and leadership

AIMS
A To examine relevant skills for virtual leadership
B To develop skills for motivating and involving
C To consider team-building in a virtual environment
D To analyse how culture affects leaders and teams

A Discussion and listening

Think about it

> *How can I manage them if I can't see them?*
> Elizabeth Lee Kelley,
> Senior Lecturer in Programme
> and Project Management,
> Cranfield Business School

1 **Do you need to be able to see people to manage them? What is your own experience of leading people, either face to face or virtually? What differences in leadership qualities do you think are needed?**

2 a **What influence could these factors have on the way a virtual manager leads a group?**
- geographical distance
- cultural differences
- functional speciality
- age
- competing demands
- personalities
- time differences

b **Can you think of any other factors that might also have an effect?**

Listen to this

3 🎧 41 **Martina Schneider, a consultant, is discussing with a colleague some of the qualities required in virtual leadership. Listen to the first part of the conversation and answer these questions.**
a What is the key factor Martina mentions at the beginning?
b What two things does Martina mention that a leader can observe in face-to-face meetings?
c What three qualities does Martina use as examples of how a leader can model positive behaviour?
d Why is it important for a leader to monitor the activities of virtual team members?

4 🎧 42 **Listen to the second part of Martina's talk and answer these questions.**
a What two questions does Martina say leaders need to ask regarding expectations?
b Why do virtual team members need to be reminded of 'the big picture'?
c What two examples of leadership styles in virtual teams does Martina give?

5 **If you had to deal with the problems mentioned as examples by Martina, what would you do?**

Focus on language

6 Match the two halves of the sentences (1–8 and a–h) to give recommendations on how virtual team leaders can establish a healthy working environment for their teams.

Example: 1 a

1 Building and maintaining harmonious one-to-one
2 Giving personal feedback on an individual's
3 Managing local issues affecting individuals in different
4 Storing and retrieving data and documentation in
5 Providing specific and rapid responses to immediate
6 Collecting different information from individuals so
7 Mediating conflict between two team
8 Maximising use of combined team expertise by using an online

a relationships by having frequent personal contact.
b a location known to everyone.
c the whole team can access that knowledge base.
d discussion forum to encourage a collaborative culture.
e time zones by contacting them at suitable times.
f members by working to minimise their differences.
g performance and offering training where necessary.
h problems by being available at short notice.

7 Choose a verb / verbs from the box that can be used with each set of nouns / noun phrases below.

| build   inspire/create   maximise   mediate |
| provide/offer   store   train/develop |

a ..*build*........ relationships / networks / team spirit / rapport / mutual trust
b .... conflict / disputes / arguments / disagreements
c .... team members / skills sets / good practices
d .... guidance / assistance / help / advice / solutions
e .... data / documents / files / e-mails / knowledge
f .... trust / loyalty / goodwill / allegiance / team spirit
g .... synergies / individual expertise / opportunities / involvement

Let's talk

8 a Read this list of possible qualities for a virtual leader. In groups, discuss how relevant you think each quality is and rank them in order of importance.

- a strong and dominant personality
- availability at any time of the day or night
- knowledge and experience of global cultural differences
- capacity to identify and adapt to different communication styles
- good communicator by telephone
- expert user of all forms of communication technology

b Which other qualities could be important? Discuss in your groups and add to the list.

B Communication skills: Skills for motivating and involving

Think about it 1 Bruce Tuckman, Professor of Educational Psychology at Ohio State University in the US, created a team model identifying the different phases in the lifecycle of a team. Match each of his stages (1–4) with its definition (a–d).
1 forming   2 storming   3 norming   4 performing

a Having one goal and coming to a mutual plan, with the ambition to work for the success of the team's goals
b Functioning as a unit to get the job done smoothly and effectively without inappropriate conflict or the need for external supervision
c Different ideas competing for consideration, such as what problems the members of the team are really supposed to solve, how they will function independently and together, and what leadership model they will accept
d Initial behaviour is driven by a desire to be accepted by the others, and avoid controversy or conflict. Serious issues and feelings are avoided, and people focus on being busy with routines, such as team organisation.

2 Which of the four stages could be the most challenging for a virtual team? Does a virtual leader need to lead in a more directive or 'autocratic' way? Why? / Why not?

Listen to this 3 a 🎧 43 Dermott Shaughnessy is holding a pre-project conference call with his newly formed team. At the beginning of the call, Dermott uses four words to describe the positive consequences of operating with a common understanding. What are they?

b According to Dermott's 'team clock' model, what messages do the following clock faces represent?

c How often will Dermott adjust the clock?

4 🎧 44 Listen to the second part of Dermott's call and choose the best option(s) in each case.
a Dermott believes that having teams in four continents makes tasks:
   i) more interesting.   ii) easier.   iii) more complicated.   iv) faster.
b Which two of these aspects of virtual teamwork does Dermott *not* mention?
   i) knowledge-sharing   ii) information processing   iii) data storage
   iv) collaboration   v) behaviour
c Dermott wants his team to look at the key elements he provides and:
   i) agree to the rules he has already decided.   ii) decide the necessary norm together.

5 What do you think of Dermott's communication style? Would you like him as a team leader? Why? / Why not?

Focus on language 6 After the conference call, Dermott encourages his team to give feedback. Complete his e-mail on page 81, using words from the box.

| allocated | charter | contributions | cross-reference | draft |
| format | involvement | minute-taker | productive | template |

80   8 Teams and leadership

From: Dermott Shaughnessy <d.shaughnessy@globalcorp.com>

Dear all,
Firstly, thanks very much to all of you for your **(a)** *contributions* to the conference call yesterday. It was very **(b)** .... , and you should have my **(c)** .... version of the team **(d)** .... for your feedback in your inboxes in a couple of hours.

I've got a few things to mention about conference calls. The biggest problem is always **(e)** .... If you aren't the one speaking, I know and you know that the temptation is to multi-task, because you know no one will notice if they can't see you.

So, what I would like to do is rotate a couple of positions of responsibility for each conference call. These responsibilities will be **(f)** .... to a different person every week. It also means I don't have to do the impossible and try to fulfil three roles during each call!

- The challenger: takes a constructively critical attitude to opinions expressed. Makes us 'tighter'.
- The **(g)** ....: records decisions – not verbatim, but not just notes either.
- The facilitator: runs the meeting – good practice for you all!

I will also be sending out an agenda to all of you. This is the **(h)** .... we can all use for writing up the minutes, so that there is always a common **(i)** .... for each document to make it easier to access or **(j)** .... information from previous conference calls.

Kind regards,
Dermott

---

7 Many word partnerships can be used to talk about important factors in virtual teamwork. Look at the key words in bold and the words or phrases that commonly come before them. Then complete each of the sentences below with an appropriate word partnership.

1 establish / standardised / lack of / specific / achievable / define	**aims /goals**
2 rude / collaborative / respectful / obstructive / conflictive / positive	**attitude**
3 follow / observe / ignore / agreed / strict / recommended	**norms**
4 allocate / keep to / waste / run out of / limit / response	**time**
5 foreign / technical / ambiguous / explicit / understandable / native	**language**

a If we don't .... the .... about turn-taking, this call will take far too long!

b Your .... is seen as .... because you seem to enjoy starting arguments.

c Those of us using our own language need to speak slower and more clearly for those of us who are not ....-..................... speakers.

d This project is problematic because there are no .... , so no one knows what output we are moving towards.

e Everyone should .... the .... they speak during calls, otherwise some people won't get the chance to intervene.

f Hello, everyone. The purpose of this kick-off call is to .... the .... of the project and to get to know each other a little.

g I think it's better to approach this problem with a .... rather than being pessimistic about its magnitude!

Let's talk **8** Think of someone you think is a good leader. Tell a partner what qualities makes that person so good.

9 Good leaders do many of these things. In groups, rank the importance of each of the actions when working in a virtual team.

- allocating roles
- celebrating success
- coaching or mentoring by phone
- criticising incorrect action
- delegating responsibility
- emphasising deadlines
- giving all individuals equal treatment
- requesting daily updates

8 Teams and leadership

C Professional skills: Team-building in a virtual environment

Think about it

1 An employee survey of multinational companies from 77 countries asked what qualities make a good virtual colleague. The responses are shown below. Of the seven categories, which do you feel you are good at, and which do you need to improve on in order to be a better virtual teammate?

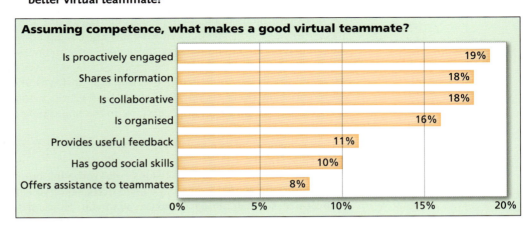

2 How might the skills for virtual team members be different to those of regular team members? How might the percentages in the chart above reflect these differences?

Read this

3 The article on page 83 emphasises key qualities for virtual team members. Read it, then match each heading (a–f) with the correct paragraph (1–6).
   a Be an ambassador
   b Learn the rules of the road
   c Be self-aware
   d Manage your expectations
   e Reach out your hand
   f Go to school

4 Read the article again and answer these questions.
   a Why could humour be dangerous?
   b When should goals, roles and responsibilities be clearly established?
   c If there are no clear, established protocols for communication, what should happen?
   d What outside factors can influence an individual's performance?
   e What should team members do if they are not strong with a particular communication technology?
   f Can core skills be transferred to different projects?

5 The article talks about *strong collaborative skills*. How easy is it for individuals to develop these skills? Share your experiences with a partner.

Focus on language

6 Match each of the key qualities for team members (1–8) with the best ending (a–h).
   1 Responsiveness
   2 Observance
   3 Adaptability
   4 Collaboration
   5 Responsibility
   6 Ownership
   7 Knowledge
   8 Willingness

   a with others on shared tasks, knowledge sharing
   b of essential virtual collaboration skills and team tools
   c to invitations, urgent requests or requirements from others
   d of your task completion, performance and priorities
   e for taking tough decisions
   f of norms for timeliness, co-operation and response
   g to change work schedule at short notice
   h to global demands and constraints

7 Complete these sentences with the verb form of the key qualities in Exercise 6.
   a He must be flexible and try to .... to changes in his working environment.
   b If we don't .... with each other, the project will fail.
   c We all need to be committed – to really .... our individual project briefs.

8 Teams and leadership

How to be an artful collaborator

1 ....
Take responsibility for what you contribute to the team environment. Your tone of voice, writing style, responsiveness and overall openness to working with others that may work in different ways are all important factors in artful collaboration. Be especially careful how you use humour – a powerful ice-breaker, but also a dangerous one because people from different cultures may not find the same things funny. Furthermore, if you don't understand the joke, you may feel excluded.

2 ....
Get clear on the team's goal and the roles and responsibilities of all members, not just your own. Ask any clarifying questions as soon as appropriate to ensure you and all members have a common understanding. Recommendation: If you are a team leader, present these items in a kick-off real-time call or web meeting followed by sharing the key documents on the team collaboration site. Schedule a follow-up call after the team members have had time to digest the information. If you are a team member, recommend these steps to the leader.

3 ....
Understand and follow the procedures and guidelines for communicating, sharing documents, and reporting status. Use the designated tools, be timely in frequency of posts, be responsive to queries, and let others know how to best contact you. If there are no clear, established protocols for communication, work with the team leader and members to establish them! Take into consideration the varying time zones, cultural norms, as well as project goals when choosing how the group agrees to proceed.

4 ....
Be aware of the pressures and priorities outside of the team which may impact team members, including yourself. Take the time to get to know your teammates, their cultural, organisational and/or functional differences. Share ideas, thoughts and inspiration. Make an effort to appreciate each member's strengths and uniqueness.

5 ....
Take time to become comfortable with all of the collaboration and communication tools used by the team. Seek extra help if you are new to a tool or a way of communicating. Tap into the other team members' strengths if they seem to be better at using the tools than you.

6 ....
Welcome new members when they join. Offer to give them a 'tour' of the virtual space and brief them on the activities and accomplishments to date. Introduce team members to one another. Having strong collaborative skills is a competitive advantage in the virtual and global workplace. Each individual contributor on a virtual collaborative team deals with unique challenges for each new project or team they join. Building these core skills will help you to become an artful collaborator and put you in higher demand.

adapted from an article by Linda DeLuca, business advisor and coach founder of Azione-Scopo

d It's vital that the team leader .... to their team's doubts sympathetically.
e Sometimes it's better to listen and .... a situation rather than to make assumptions.
f .... you .... to work overtime tonight? I'd really appreciate it.
g He .... every aspect of our virtual dashboard system like the back of his hand!
h I .... not .... for the mistakes of other people!

Let's talk   **8**   Work with a partner. You are members of a committee in charge of an international humanitarian project in Africa. This requires teamwork across five continents and a special kind of leadership to oversee and co-ordinate the activities of local team leaders. Your line manager has drawn up a shortlist of four candidates for the position of team leader, and they want your recommendations on the best candidate.

Student A: Turn to page 93.
Student B: Turn to page 94.

Exchange information about the two different candidate profiles you each have. Once you have information on all four candidates, discuss their merits and decide on the best one.

9 What influenced your decision? Did you agree at first? Which qualities and competences were most important?

D Intercultural competence: How culture affects leaders and teams

1 What is your experience of working in a culturally diverse team? How, if at all, did you prepare for this diversity? How would the challenges have differed if the team had only been working virtually?

2 The chart below shows more results from the survey you saw on page 82, where respondents were asked to rank the challenges from most to least difficult. How far do the challenges you face personally when working virtually compare with these findings? Are there any challenges which are not mentioned in the survey which you feel are important? Discuss with a partner.

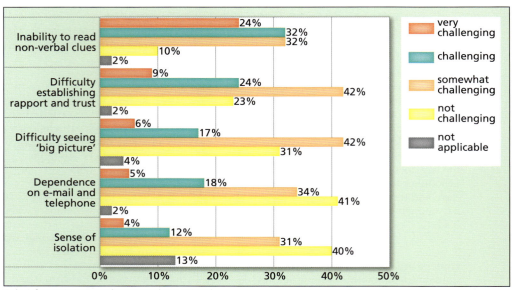

Taken from 2012 survey by RW3 Culture Wizard

3 Professor Geert Hofstede is a leading thinker and researcher into cross-cultural communication. He conducted one of the most comprehensive studies ever about how values in the workplace are influenced by culture. He is recognised internationally for having developed the first model of 'dimensions' of national culture, establishing a new way of measuring the effect of cultural factors on international economics, communication and co-operation.
One of the five cultural dimensions he modelled was Individualism versus Collectivism. As he defined it:

The degree of interdependence a society maintains among its members has to do with whether people's self-image is defined in terms of 'I' or 'we'. In Individualist societies, people are supposed to look after themselves and their direct family only. In Collectivist societies, people belong to 'in groups' that take care of them in exchange for loyalty.

The four cultures described below and on page 85 illustrate some of the key attributes of this cultural dimension. Can you think of four countries which could match the four descriptions? Discuss your opinions with your partner.

Culture A: This is amongst the most individualistic. Children are socialised from an early age, and are taught to think for themselves, to find out what their unique purpose in life is and how they can contribute to society, whilst benefiting themselves. The route to happiness is through personal fulfilment. As the affluence of this country has increased over the last 30 years, there has been a rise in consumerism, a fall in the observance of traditional religious values and a strengthening of the 'me' culture.

Culture B: Within Europe, this culture is considered as highly collectivist, due to its frequently expressed and strong sense of national identity. However, compared with other areas of the world, it is quite individualist. Teamwork is considered entirely natural, although management of team members is individual, and explicit recognition of individual contributions is expected. Employees tend to work well with no need for strong external motivation.

Culture C: This culture scores high on the individualistic index. This means that people favour individual and private opinions, taking care of themselves and immediate family rather than belonging to a group. Work relationships are contract-based, the focus is on the task, and a high acceptance of individual autonomy is normal. Communication is mostly direct, and everyone is allowed to voice opinions, especially if they do not agree.

Culture D: This is a highly collectivist culture, where people act in the interests of the group and not necessarily of themselves. Decisions affecting recruitment are often closely linked to family, community and personal contacts. Employee commitment to the organisation is often high, and relationships with colleagues are co-operative, supportive and team-oriented. Personal relationships can be as important as the task and company, and it is regarded as important not to 'lose face'.

adapted from http://geert-hofstede.com/countries.html

4 How can a team leader with members from the four different cultures described in Exercise 3 ensure that the virtual team can work to its full potential?

Case study: EasyFix

Background EasyFix is an automotive company specialising in spare parts for the car-leasing industry. It is based in the UK, but has partnerships with manufacturers in France and distributors in Spain and Portugal. The founding company was American. The US firm no longer has much influence over business decisions, but the management style is dominant and top-down, with the focus on short-term results. Like all its competitors, EasyFix is suffering from falling sales due to the continuing recession in Europe and it is under pressure from its shareholders to improve performance.

Situation The Sales Manager, Jayne, has been instructed by the Head of European Sales to set up a new initiative designed to increase the sales contracts secured by her team each month. Jayne knows that most of her team are feeling extremely demotivated. They are very worried by the lack of demand in their countries due to the economic situation. However, despite the current situation, Jayne is determined to maintain a positive mood and engage her team fully in the new initiative.

Tasks 1 🎧 45 Listen to an extract from the conference call, which Jayne organises to launch the initiative. Make notes on the behaviour displayed during the call.

2 Discuss these questions.
   a What cultural issues are highlighted by Jayne's call?
   b What should Jayne's priorities be after this meeting?
   c What action would you take in her position?

E Language reference

Read through the key words and phrases below from this unit. Add any other useful words and expressions which you feel are important for you to learn. Make sure you find the time to review these words and phrases regularly and to use them at work.

Word partnerships for virtual leadership tasks
local (management) demands
local constraints
build relationships/trust/respect
manage (local) issues/problems/incidents
provide response(s)/guidance
gather information/opinions/viewpoints
maximise expertise/engagement/involvement
delegate tasks/responsibilities/authority

Leadership qualities

presence	flexibility
responsiveness	predictability
persuasiveness	adaptability
inclusiveness	decisiveness

Word partnerships for team management
team charter/norms/guidelines/collaboration
standardised practice(s) / procedures / response times
draft document/report/e-mail/response
to cross-reference documents/information/sources

Conference-call roles
timekeeper
minute-taker
facilitator

Language for making suggestions
How about keeping this item until the end of the call?
Why don't we wait until she replies to the message?
Let's have a five-minute time-out – we've been on the line for two hours.
I think it would be a good idea to confirm completion of this phase.
We (really) should take prompt action on his comments.
You ought to apologise for what you said to him during the call.

Leader language for managing tasks and team
What I would like you to do is …
Please let me know …
I expect all of you to …
I will be sending you … Please confirm you have received it.
I'd (really) appreciate it if you could (all) …
Everyone should …
I think it's better if we (all) …
(Please) do not …

Writing task Choose one or both of the following writing activities. Integrate at least five standard expressions from above into the e-mail(s) of your choice.
1 Write an e-mail to your virtual team to introduce yourself as their team leader. Tell them what you expect of them in terms of collaboration and how you would like them to communicate with each other during the project they will be working on together.
2 You are having problems keeping in contact with your teammate in Venezuela because of time differences and their work routine. Write an e-mail to this teammate suggesting a solution to this issue.

F Virtual working tips and personal action plan

1 **Take a few minutes to reflect on these tips for relationship-building. Which do you think is the most important, and which ideas are most useful?**

TIP 1

Engage team members by ensuring they play an active role in the processes and procedures. This involvement must be meaningful for it to be truly effective.
Ideas for engaging:
- Rotating the roles during a call is a very effective way of engaging at least a few of your team members. It will keep everyone involved and reduce the risk of people not giving their full attention.
- Before a conference call, make a brief note to yourself to remind you that certain individuals may need more encouragement to contribute than others.

TIP 2

Use face-to-face time with virtual team members effectively to build stronger relationships. Create opportunities for people to socialise together and learn more about the component parts of their team.
Ideas for building relationships:
- Talk in depth to each individual member to discover more about their style, motivations and local constraints. It will help you understand how they like to approach the process of virtual teamworking. Encourage individuals to exchange ideas, too.
- Set aside time at the beginning of a meeting for the team to present themselves using a single slide. The visual images will be more effective reminders to most people.

TIP 3

Demonstrate in a consistent way the kind of behaviour you want your team to aspire to. If you act in a positive way, others under your authority will copy, or 'mirror', that behaviour, therefore creating a positive dynamic throughout the group in question.
Ideas for modeling behaviour:
- Stick to your agenda, be a good time-keeper and observe the communication guidelines you have agreed on.
- Give feedback which is affirmative and developmental rather than critical.
- Be flexible in your communication style and welcome diversity.

Personal action plan 2 **Think about what you have learned from this unit. Note down two or three important points which you want to apply to your own job (*What?*). Then create a schedule to implement your learning (*When?*) and think about the best way to check that you have successfully applied these ideas (*How?*).**

3 **Discuss your action plan and adapt it if necessary, based on any useful feedback you get.**

	what I learned and want to apply to my job	when/how I will apply this in my job	how I will check if I have applied it
1			
2			
3			

8 Teams and leadership

Activity file

Unit 3, Communication skills, Exercise 10

Student A
You are the IT Manager. Your task is to:
- defend your department's budget – you make the company run smoothly!
- justify why you need to renovate office hardware and invest in tablet devices.
- indicate why there should be an increase in the training budget.
- suggest that the company could save money in the long term if people knew how to use computers properly – they don't listen to you!

Take a few minutes to prepare your arguments. The meeting will be chaired by the Finance Manager and(s)he will have the final word.

Unit 5, Discussion and listening, Exercise 10

Look at this 'To do' list. Discuss which is the most appropriate channel in each case and then use the table below to note the advantages and disadvantages you find.

To do
a Check the time of the next weekly team meeting.
b Wish your colleague in the office on the next floor a happy birthday.
c Contact a colleague who has been using your materials in his presentation and pretending they are his own, and let him know how annoyed you feel.
d Explain to the IT help desk that their suggestions on how to fix your computer did not work.
e Get directions from a customer on how to find their new headquarters.
f Share the good news that your company is to introduce a profit-share scheme with your whole team.
g Ask a member of your team to come to a disciplinary meeting to discuss an incident which happened yesterday.

communication channel	task (a–g)	advantages	disadvantages
phone			
SMS			
e-mail			
IM			
social media			
face-to-face			

Unit 7, Communication skills, Exercise 9

Student A
You represent the global R&D department.
The product was developed after long and complex work to create a unique product for the market. You don't want to see all the department's hard work go to waste. The pilot results are mixed, but you think the company should:
- allow you to make some further small changes to this new product – it is very close to having a truly global attraction to millions of consumers
- maintain (or even increase?) the R&D budget, as you are very near to achieving a real breakthrough in developing a range of new lines based on the work you have done on this product
- work with the production team to implement more flexible and efficient production processes for this and other products.

Unit 5, Language reference

E-mail templates
A simple way to improve the accuracy of your e-mails is to prepare model frameworks which you can reuse many times with minor changes of words and facts. Take a look at these examples and simply adapt them to your needs.

Organising a meeting
I am writing to arrange our next P12 meeting to discuss the new sales strategy for eastern Europe. I would propose 13:00–18:00 on 15 January in Berlin.
Please let me know as soon as possible if these dates are convenient.

Confirming a meeting
Thank you for the meeting invitation. I can confirm that 15 January is convenient for me. Could you please book a room for me at the Hilton, as usual?
I look forward to seeing you.

Requesting information
I am writing to request a copy of your latest catalogue of management training products. Please could you also send me information on your language training courses?

Explaining a problem
I am having problems accessing my e-mail from my desktop. When I click to open my mailbox, the screen freezes and I have to reboot.
Please could you solve this problem as soon as possible?

Solving a problem
This access problem was caused by a configuration error. Please use NEWSYSTEM as a password next time you access your mailbox.
If you have any further problems, please contact me immediately.

Unit 3, Communication skills, Exercise 10

Student B
You are the HR Manager. Your task is to:
- ask for an increase to your department's budget for training, as you think it's too low.
- justify why there should not be a reduction in the number of office-based PCs – they are necessary.
- indicate why the IT department should be more efficient in its training programmes.
- argue strongly against any cuts that the Finance Manager suggests: the company's performance will suffer.

Take a few minutes to prepare your arguments. The meeting will be chaired by the Finance Manager and (s)he will have the final word.

Unit 6, Discussion and listening, Exercise 9a

origin/birthplace Where are you from? Where were you born?	family circumstances Have you got any children? Are you married/single?	interests, hobbies or passions (professional/personal) Are you interested in …? What do you like –ing?
speciality/position What (exactly) do you do?	virtual working experience Have you ever …? How long have you worked …?	your work experience in general What jobs have you had? How long …?
experiences, interests of professional areas in common I … . How about you?	hopes, expectations and ambitions What are your hopes for …? What do you want to do when …?	your use of technology Do you use social media? What devices …?

Unit 6, Intercultural competence, Exercise 4

Student A
Situation 1
Your remote team leader keeps on dumping extra work on you without much warning. They insist that it is required the next morning. These tasks are not your responsibility, but always seem to be urgent.
You have always helped them out without complaining, but they seem to have no idea of all the other work you have to do for your local line manager. They seem unaware of the pressure this puts on you. You think your team leader is taking advantage of your goodwill.
You are really stressed and a little angry. Prepare to receive a call from your team leader (Student B) and defend your position.

Situation 2
You need to speak to a virtual team member (Student B) about performance. They aren't substandard – in fact, they are very competent – but their actions in relation to other team members are chaotic; lack of punctuality, incorrect documents, failure to respond in a timely way to requests and a general lack of personal organisational capacity. It affects relationships and effectiveness throughout the team.
You are calling this person to find out what the problem is and to make it clear the situation is unacceptable.

Unit 7, Communication skills, Exercise 9

Student B
You represent the marketing department in market X.
The pilot has been a great success in your country, where the market is highly competitive and consumers are always on the lookout for the next new thing.
You think the company should:
- start large-scale production as soon as possible to satisfy the obvious demand
- devise a marketing strategy which pushes the product aggressively, with celebrity endorsement and a wide-ranging set of promotional activities
- recruit an experienced brand manager to direct operations for this big push.

Unit 7, Communication skills, Exercise 10

	The meeting was effective because …	yes	no
1	the purpose and goals of the meeting were clear.		
2	everyone gave their opinions.		
3	all participants respected each other and gave each other a chance to speak.		
4	it was not dominated by one or two people.		
5	it was exactly the right length – not too long and not too short.		
6	we kept to the topic all the time.		
7	the leader of the meeting had good control of the participants, topic and timing.		
8	we all behaved professionally and didn't make personal remarks.		
9	our knowledge of English was sufficient to understand most of it.		
10	other:		

Unit 3, Communication skills, Exercise 10

Student C
You are the Sales Manager. Your task is to:
- reduce the number of office-based PCs.
- suggest tablet computers for all sales staff, as they are out in the field most of the time.
- move towards having more tablet apps and fewer big software suites, which are a waste of money.
- remind people that all the company's laptops are outdated and slow. You want replacements.

Take a few minutes to prepare your arguments. The meeting will be chaired by the Finance Manager and (s)he will have the final word.

Unit 6, Intercultural competence, Exercise 4

Student B
Situation 1
You manage Student A remotely. You have been very overworked recently. There are some very important tasks you have not had time to do yourself, so you have been leaving them for Student A to do. Student A is a highly competent, hard-working and trusted member of your team.
Today, another task has come up and you need Student A's help.
These tasks are not really part of Student A's job description, but they are important, so you feel they should not mind doing them for you, to help you out in a crisis.
Call Student A and persuade them to do the work.

Situation 2
You joined the organisation nine months ago and you joined this virtual team shortly after. You feel you are doing too much work at present. Your local line manager is not happy that you cannot fulfill your obligations to the local office, and you strongly feel that the virtual team manager is expecting too much of you.
Why don't they share the tasks among the whole team? You do not like to be singled out as a 'special' individual. Prepare to receive a call from your virtual project manager (Student A).

Unit 7, Communication skills, Exercise 9

Student C

You represent the production department in market Y.

In your market, the pilot has been disappointing, as there are established brands with similar drinks, and you do not feel optimistic about establishing the company in this market segment. You think the company should:
- concentrate on its existing cash-cow products in your market
- avoid producing large quantities of this product, as it is unlikely to sell well
- go back to production development and work on adapting the product to create more of a USP. It could be a good product, but changes are needed.

Unit 8, Professional skills, Exercise 8

Student A

CANDIDATE 1
Name: Majeed Khan (Pakistan)
Age: 37
Experience: Seven years leading outsourced teams in Indian sub-continent; led virtual project last year with eight team members
Comments: Charismatic, brilliant but not always reliable, very direct in communication, outspoken in meetings, sees himself as a born leader, expects high standards, very ambitious, cricket fanatic

CANDIDATE 2
Name: Weiping Xao (China)
Age: 41
Experience: 12 years in international teams in China and SE Asia; based in Shanghai; travels locally a lot; has never led virtual project, but keen to widen experience and work globally; reliable and autonomous; taking classes to improve English
Comments: Respected, dedicated, demanding of others, a little serious, says little in meetings: 'actions speak louder than words'

Unit 3, Communication skills, Exercise 10

Student D

You are the Finance Manager. Your task is to:
- lead the meeting. Make sure everyone participates equally.
- justify why there should be cuts in IT and training budgets because of efficiency measures.
- say that you think 'hot-desking' is better than fixed office-based PCs.
- say that you think training has always been a waste of time because people never attend, and courses are too general.

Take a few minutes to prepare for the call. You will have the final word. Appoint one of the other three participants to take minutes.

Unit 8, Professional skills, Exercise 8

Student B

CANDIDATE 3
Name: Jana Kopecky (Czech Republic)
Age: 32
Experience: Ten years in international teams; widely travelled; limited virtual team experience, but frequent phone contact with suppliers in Latin America; single mother, two children, wants to work from home some of the time
Comments: Popular, sociable, lots of energy, can bring out the best in others if encouraged, a little quiet in large groups

CANDIDATE 4
Name: Harold Sharp (UK)
Age: 45
Experience: Ten years in international teams; widely travelled; led small virtual project last year with three team members; very knowledgeable in the sector; doing PhD part-time
Comments: Well-liked, team-player, humorous, a little 'absent-minded' at times, ex-teacher, brings out the best in others, doesn't say much in meetings, prefers written communication

Unit 7, Communication skills, Exercise 9

Student D

You represent the finance department in market Z.
You were sceptical about this product, and quite honestly, the pilot has been a disaster in your market. The taste has had very negative feedback in blind-testing on consumers. You think the company should:
- reject any further development of this product, as it has been very expensive
- move in a different direction and start copying some of your main competitor's product lines. It's cheaper, and the return on investment is much faster
- realise that the R&D department's budget should be cut in these difficult times – money doesn't grow on trees!

Audio script

UNIT 1

Track 1
Bettina: I'm Bettina, a project manager responsible for a team which is testing materials for protecting cars. My colleagues are all over the world, but we have frequent contact, either by e-mail or instant messaging. This is useful for collaboration, such as finding solutions to problems. We have a weekly full-team conference call, where we exchange ideas and opinions about the project. I think we could save time just sending written documents, updates and reminders to individual team members rather than wasting time explaining them. If I need a quick update, I use Skype.

Track 2
Ana: I'm Ana, the team leader for a group of programmers for a telecoms company. We design and develop software, running a strict testing programme to analyse results. I also try to achieve agreement on our objectives and guarantee that we meet deadlines. Although my team members work worldwide, we all get the job done efficiently. It helped that I invested time at the beginning, building strong relationships with each team member. Conference calls are short but frequent, every couple of days. Otherwise, we phone and e-mail each other about progress. Conference calls are useful – we achieve a lot and we have social conversations as well. We share documents and updates and we also write and edit reports together. My team is a very pleasant and committed group of individuals! We've discovered a lot about each other, and because the atmosphere is friendly, we perform well.

Track 3
Chantou: I'm Chantou. I'm a factory manager in the city of Guangzhou. We … work with two other plants: one in Switzerland and another in the USA. We supply machinery … and parts for food manufacturing. I send e-mails every day, and I use my phone to send photos of operational problems. We have conference calls every … Tuesday. I have to report to my senior managers about production issues. I never learned English when I was at school, so my colleagues are difficult to understand. Um, I don't like conference calls very much – um … I worry because I cannot … um … communicate well.
I am working in a technical area, and I give details and pictures. Often, um, most of the meeting content is not relevant to me, so sometimes I don't attend conference calls because they are at night.

Track 4
Interviewer: Tell me something about yourself and your experiences of working virtually.
Jorma: I'm Jorma, a senior lecturer at the University of Applied Sciences in Helsinki. Teaching virtually has become a regular feature of my timetable because the geographical and work-related demands on mature students mean many courses involve an element of distance learning. I meet my students face to face only once every seven or eight weeks.
Interviewer: What factors do you need to bear in mind when you carry out distance classes?
Jorma: Well, firstly, there are technological challenges. To run a class effectively, the teacher needs a webcam, a headset microphone and a software program like Connect Pro. The technical side is not very demanding – the most common problem I experience is with the microphone. Then, of course, you have to think about your voice, the pace of delivery and how long you can keep your students' attention!
Interviewer: Mm, I see.
Jorma: Finns tend to be softly spoken, they don't like to draw attention to themselves, so I've had to train myself to speak much louder, be clearer and more direct when expressing myself to avoid misunderstandings. I've also had to consider how fast I speak. To keep everyone on board, I need to create a lively atmosphere, but in general, Finns like to have much more time to reflect than other nationalities, so I also have to be careful not to put my students under pressure to come up with answers too quickly.

Track 5
Interviewer: So, Jorma, what are the challenges of teaching in this way?
Jorma: Knowing whether your class is following you is an issue. At regular intervals, you need to say things like: 'Can each person confirm they follow me?' Experience has taught me to check student understanding more frequently when teaching virtually. Similarly, I use questions like 'Is that clear?' or 'Any problems so far?' to encourage my class to ask for clarification, because this can also be a challenge. They normally say 'What exactly do you mean by …' and I soon realise that I've not been as precise as I should have! Actually, at the beginning of term, we designed our own set of rules for virtual sessions so that the whole class felt comfortable learning this way. It's essential to create a good virtual learning environment.
Interviewer: Yes.
Jorma: Obviously, some students need more encouragement than others, and I'm aware of who they are. I tend to ask these particular students either

to summarise what I've just said, using phrases like 'so, in other words' … er, or I say something like 'Rikke, we haven't heard your views on this subject yet.'

Track 6
Conversation 1

Erik: Hello?
Mercedes: Hey, Erik, how's it going?
Erik: Hello, Mercedes. Yes … fine, thanks.
Mercedes: Great! I had a great weekend waterskiing up in Cancún. You enjoy yours?
Erik: Not bad, thanks … not bad. Thank you for calling back. Um, I wanted to ask you about the Helsinki pilot programme.
Mercedes: Er, yeah, sure, Erik. What d'you wanna know? I got the primary results, and they look really positive. I think we can get a lot of usage out of the figures, and they're applicable to other areas too, especially the drag factors. It's all good! We could involve the people in Canada on this too … You still there, amigo?
Erik: Yes, yes … Well, OK. Um … I wanted to look at the wind tunnel averages … You know, the resistance capacities. Do you have them?
Mercedes: Mm, not right now, maybe it's better if I send them. Good to hear your voice, anyway. It's been a long time.
Erik: Yes … yes, it has been two months. Maybe you can send me the averages soon and then I can analyse them and … er—
Mercedes: Sure, Erik! I'll do it later. What do you think about the data mining?
Erik: Mmm …
Mercedes: Erik? You still there? Hello?
Erik: Yes, yes, Mercedes … I am just thinking.
Mercedes: What?
Erik: Huh? … No, I was thinking … about the data …
Mercedes: Huh! I thought you'd gone!

Track 7
Conversation 2

Haruka: Hello?
Monica: … Hello? … Hello? … Good morning, Haruka.
Haruka: Hello, Monica! How are you? How is Munich today?
Monica: Sorry? … Bad line … What did you say? How is …? What?
Haruka: Er … Munich. You are in Munich today, no?
Monica: Oh, yes! Yes. Sorry! It's good. Munich is OK today.
Haruka: Oh, you are lucky. Here in Osaka it's raining all morning.
Monica: Ah … right … OK. Do you want to begin, Haruka? We have a fair amount to cover.
Haruka: Yes, it's quite cold, but I hope—
Monica: We can start when you're ready.
Haruka: Sorry?
Monica: We can begin cross-checking the findings and data, OK?
Haruka: OK … OK, Monica. Well, um, I don't …
Monica: Problem?
Haruka: I was thinking … er … Can we first discuss the broad implications of the findings? … um … because … er … I do not have a detailed run-down of, er …
Monica: Um, if you want … It's just, er …
Haruka: Er … I don't have the specifics with me. Here.
Monica: Yes, I understand. But I have an analysis which we spent a lot of time on in the last two days. We don't have a lot of time, Haruka. You know, we need to move. The deadline is looming.
Haruka: Sorry? Looking?
Monica: Loom… you know, er, it's very soon.
Haruka: Er … Yes … I see …
Monica: We need to take this forward today. Is this OK, Haruka?
Haruka: Well … I don't … um, OK, Monica. OK. Can you give me five minutes and I can get my papers? Maybe we can screen-share the files?
Monica: Not necessary, really. We can just talk them through. I'll call you back in five, OK?
Haruka: Sorry?
Monica: In five minutes, I'll call you. Will you be ready then?
Haruka: Um, yes, Monica, I will. Thank you.
Monica: OK, five minutes, then.

UNIT 2

Track 8
Before any kind of communication takes place, it's essential to dedicate some time to *preparation* in order to maximise the outcomes and avoid wasting time. This includes deciding on the timing of a meeting, drawing up an agenda, circulating relevant information and, above all, making your expectations of others clear from the start.

Make sure everyone understands the *purpose* of your communication. State clearly why you are doing something, even if it seems obvious to you. Also try to give others as many opportunities as possible to check and confirm their understanding of the purpose of the communication.

Go through the *process* step by step to emphasise the way you would like people to interact, how you would like actions to be carried out and any follow-up you expect. Before you begin any kind of virtual communication, think carefully about the *people* you are about to communicate with. How will they respond to your communication style? Adopting a flexible and open approach to the way other people communicate always achieves better results, but applying this flexibility when you're communicating virtually is not easy, not easy at all, and takes a great deal of practice.

Track 9
Welcome, everyone. This afternoon's session is designed to help you plan virtual meetings so that they run more efficiently. The longer you prepare, the better your meetings should be!

So, the first point to consider is your audience. Think about how much these people know about the subject being discussed, its relevance to them – i.e. do they really need to be there? – and finally, what is their relationship to each other?

In short, plan only to invite those who really need to be there and circulate all the relevant information well ahead of the meeting to give people time to prepare.

If people don't know each other, it's a good idea when drawing up the agenda to allow time at the beginning of the meeting for small talk.

To ensure the best outcome from your meeting, you must think carefully beforehand about how to keep everyone focused equally. This may mean making a mental note of those who usually don't say much and aiming to include them specifically. Right, moving on, I want to …

Track 10

… deal with this during the call. So, once you have drawn up your agenda, circulated the necessary support documents, such as presentation slides, and thought about who you should invite, the next step is to decide on when to hold the meeting. Don't forget to take into account the different time zones people may be working in. Ideally, you should plan to alternate meeting times so that everyone shares some of the inconvenient timing. That way, people are less likely to feel resentful about meeting late at night.

It's also important to consider beforehand what rules you want to introduce at the beginning of the meeting in order to minimise disruption. For example, will people be allowed to use instant messaging? Do you want the mute button to be used?

Finally, I recommend you take time to test the technology before the meeting or request that everyone dial in ten minutes early to sort out any minor problems with sound, for example. A good virtual facilitator makes sure they are familiar with their equipment and always has a back-up plan in case the technology fails. OK, any questions? Yes, Paolo …

UNIT 3

Track 11

Interviewer: Karen, I understand your team is based all over the world and so it's critical that everybody is kept up to date on what's happening. The projects you work on are often fast-moving and very costly to run.

Karen: Yes … not only that, many of our projects are interrelated, and it's vital that things run smoothly and that deadlines are respected. I need to be able to contact any of my team at short notice to discuss any issues we may face and implement changes quickly and smoothly. Our business demands that we are innovative and ahead of our competitors the whole time, and communicating ideas effectively within the team is very important.

Interviewer: I see. So how exactly do you manage this?

Karen: Well, it's not easy. The first problem is reaching people at the right time, remembering what time zone they're working in. Also, if they're on the factory floor, are they able to leave what they're doing and take part in a telco? After all, a factory manager's first concern is his production line! Apart from that, if you want to set up a telco, you need to prepare well in advance, sending out invitations, circulating the agenda and making sure that the technology works. Our conference suite in the head office is amazing, but that doesn't mean we won't have problems with sound or logging in on the day!

Interviewer: Tell me more about a typical call.

Karen: Telcos are usually set up to present project updates, not to discuss sudden changes which occur. Ideally, we don't use them to talk about critical issues, because telcos take time to prepare and that's something we don't have. I prefer to handle these issues via e-mail, because I can be sure that the matter is dealt with quickly and with fewer misunderstandings. The greatest challenge I have with telcos is you can never be sure that everyone has understood the issue because of the language barrier and, more importantly, the lack of visual responses.

Track 12

Karen: But going back to your original question, the main purpose is normally to update everyone on the progress of a project, to check important milestones have been reached and to discuss any doubts people may have about next steps. Often there are unforeseen delays – for example, lack of spare parts to repair specialist machinery or changes in raw materials which affect recipes.

Therefore, throughout these meetings, it's vital the facilitator checks that everyone is on the same track, key decisions are unanimous and that people can ask for clarification. No one should feel uncomfortable if they don't grasp everything first time round. We need to create an environment in which it's OK to admit you don't understand and to ask for repetition as many times as you need to, not suffer in silence!

This raises several issues, the first of which is commonly known as 'saving face', where, for example, some colleagues from Asia may say 'yes' to things they don't necessarily fully understand in order to avoid any embarrassment. The second is that someone of relative seniority cannot appear ignorant in front of their team.

The facilitator's job, then, is to summarise frequently, reducing the chances of misunderstanding and allowing for clarification and correction of inaccurate information. This is time-consuming, but in the long run, it's more effective and definitely worth it! Encouraging people to use simple words and not long, over-complex sentences is another way to avoid misunderstanding. I'm always reminding my team to keep it short and simple. After all, it's all about getting your message across as simply as you can!

Track 13

Richard: OK, four of us are here. What about François … François? Have you joined us? Hello? … François?

François: Yeah, here.

Richard: OK. Susana, *you're* there. Let's start. Um, I've put together a brief agenda, which I sent you all about 30 minutes ago. Do you all have it?
Susana: Yeah.
Jessica: Yep.
François: OK, I got it.
Richard: Imran!
Imran: What?!
Richard: Have you got the agenda?
Imran: Yeah. OK. It's in front of me, but as the person responsible for communications, I think it's really important for me to make a couple of points about our communications strategy.
Richard: Just a moment, Imran … Er, Susana, what's happening? Could you give us a status report?
Susana: OK. Right, well, we had to stop production on one of the lines because there was a positive testing for unsafe bacteria, and …
Imran: Hang on. This is Imran. When did this—
Richard: Er, Imran, just wait til Susana's finished. Susana, carry on …
Susana: We found bacteria in a sample from a batch which came off the line an hour ago.
Richard: Have you run any tests?
Susana: François, have you ordered a check on the machinery like I told you to?
François: They're doing it now. We've run several analyses on samples …
Susana: What is your risk analysis as Plant Manager?
François: The total contamination is … in … is inside the limits of acceptable levels.
Jessica: Sorry, just a minute. Sorry to interrupt, François, but this is a quality issue. We need to trace where it might have come from.
Susana: Susana here. Say that again, Jessica, the line's not so clear …
Imran: Can I just ask what I wanted to ask before?
Susana: Who's speaking now … François?
Richard: No, no, Susana. Imran just wanted to say something, but can I just remind you all. If we don't wait for each other to finish, it's very difficult to have a coherent conversation …

Track 14

François: Richard, this is François. I wanted to ask you what we're going to do about inventory in stores.
Richard: Right, François, what I think we should do is communicate internally that we need to recall all deliveries distributed in the last 24 hours, in case someone raises this at a later date. Jessica, you'll run the quality checks on all equipment and machinery at the plant—
François: Sorry, er, excuse me. Richard, just to be clear, that means all regional distribution warehouses and retail outlets – points of sale – in Benelux and Poland?
Richard: Yes. Total recall.
Susana: Well, Richard, the thing is … I know you're all worried about this, but I'm absolutely certain there's minimal risk of cross-contamination. May I remind you that the levels we found are much, much lower than the limits of what is acceptable in terms of international standards.
Imran: Susana! Just close them down! Just for the time being. Come on!
Richard: Sorry, Susana, what was that? None of us could hear.
Susana: No, nothing.
Richard: Right … Um, can I just go round and check you're all happy with that? I think we can leave it there and get on with tasks. Yes? Jessica, you've been a bit quiet this morning. Have you had the chance to say what's on your mind?
Jessica: Yes …
Richard: OK … time is critical now, so let's get moving. We have all the facts on the table and we know what to do.
Imran: OK. Is that it? What about brand protection?
Richard: That's obviously an important point, Imran, but could you and I talk about that offline after the call?
Imran: Yeah, fine. But don't leave it too long!
Richard: Er … OK. So, unless there's anything else urgently connected to this …
All: No. / Nothing else.
Richard: Right, then. Thanks for coming. Do your best, won't you?
Imran: Don't we always?!
Richard: OK. Thanks, then. Bye.

UNIT 4

Track 15
Speaker 1
Interviewer: Rohan, what development will have the greatest impact?
Rohan: I think the biggest emerging technology in relation to communicating virtually is the virtual dashboard. I really believe this is starting to normalise the way teams and groups work together across continents. A dashboard, or team board, basically allows people to access live documents and edit them; it stores data which can be easily accessed; it allows direct messaging between team members and, on some of them, there's even a kind of emotional barometer – a list of emoticons, from a happy face to an unhappy one, which lets each team member express how they feel about a situation at any moment.

Track 16
Speaker 2
Interviewer: Birgitte, how do you see the future of communications technology?
Brigitte: Since early 2012, voice-recognition programs have become increasingly sophisticated. We're reaching the point where this software is able to understand a range of accents, fast spoken language and low to high volumes with or without background noise.
Interviewer: I see.

Brigitte: This means rapid response time, more mobility and, of course, a better business result. It also means hands-free messaging, which shows us how far we have come from the typewriter!
Interviewer: Absolutely!

Track 17
Rohan: I suppose the biggest risk is that teams are, after all, human. Human error might mean that a file is not updated, or it isn't stored in the right place, and this can create real problems. Another issue is that of checking on your team's emotional well-being. I'm not convinced that asking them to use emoticons to indicate whether they are happy or sad is the best solution!

Birgitte: Well, I can see positives and negatives. One positive aspect is the variety of tasks you can complete while being able to do other things simultaneously. So, you can dictate a list while you are proofreading a document, for example. However, I do worry about the impact that all this multi-tasking will have on our capacity to concentrate on one thing at once, and I also fear an even greater avalanche of information.

Track 18
a B: So, Rohan, would you want to spend money on this product?
   R: I'm fascinated by virtual team boards and we strongly believe they need to become standard practice for all our global teams!
b R: Birgitte, how do you feel about larger business applications?
   B: I don't think the future looks positive at all for large-scale software packages. We feel they just aren't agile enough, especially for small and medium-sized businesses.
c R: So, Birgitte, do you think this voice-recognition software will become standard?
   B: Well, to be honest, I'm really not sure that the busy business executive can use this software safely to send out directions and orders – human beings make mistakes!
d R: Are we going to see the end of the written word, Birgitte?
   B: I totally disagree with people who say voice recognition eliminates the need for e-mailing – the writing process makes you think twice about the message you are sending.

Track 19
Interviewer: Alan, why is virtual communication such an attractive tool for organisations?
Alan: One of the main attractions is mobility, meaning 24/7 connectivity. Smartphones and tablet computers allow us to perform very sophisticated tasks whenever we need to and wherever we are. We can have virtual meetings, edit and share material in a variety of formats, sort out problems, collaborate or get feedback immediately on new ideas. We do all of this with a tap on a key, a swipe of a screen or even a spoken order to our device.

Interviewer: Yes, truly remarkable … but how do technological developments have an effect on communication?
Alan: Well, as fibre-optic technology makes it increasingly easier to send very large audio and data packages across cyberspace, we'll see an increase in video conferencing as the standard, rather than audio. Of course, this raises questions about how easy it is to communicate virtually with other individuals or groups. We're no longer talking about audio only, where we have no non-verbal signals to help us understand messages. The quality of streaming video is becoming better, with less time-lapse between the spoken word and the images on screen. Even so, globally, it's not uniformly stable – there are large parts of the world where internet access and broadband quality and stability are still problematic at times. And, of course, cost is still a significant factor – the more you spend, the better the technology, obviously.

Interviewer: Yeah, I see your point … Alan, do you think technology is something that distances people from each other?
Alan: Not necessarily. The same communication norms apply. We still need to get on well with people, we still share knowledge, experiences and insights. We need to collaborate and perform tasks on a daily basis. Technology can help, but we still need to use it in a way which complements the balance between good relationships and task-orientation.

Track 20
Alan: When we talk in general terms about virtual communication and technology, what we want to do in a virtual team is expressed well in this diagram, OK? So you see, we want to optimise three things regarding communication. Firstly, the results. That's the absolute bottom line! Secondly, tasks. Are we communicating with each other about tasks as efficiently and effectively as we possibly can? Thirdly, given the fact that team members rarely meet personally, we really need to make sure that our relationships are harmonious, and that we all share the same goals. Virtual teams depend on a lot of goodwill among members, so naturally getting to know people at more than just the level of someone completing a task is crucial.

OK, looking at the four influencing factors around that central point, at the top and bottom, we have synchronous and asynchronous communication. The difference is essentially that synchronous communication, such as a phone call, happens in real time, while asynchronous communication, like e-mails, is delayed. On either side of our central box, we have the other two determinants. Does the task involve simple communication or, on the other hand, is it complex communication?

Interviewer: Right. Yes … What exactly is the difference between simple and complex communication?
Alan: OK, well, simple communication means things like a quick question. Or it could be relaying specific or

small amounts of information to a group or individual. Complex communication, on the other hand, is, for instance, giving feedback to an individual team member on their performance, or making a decision about a specific issue, which requires input from several people at the same time. So, when these four factors interact with the key performance indicators of virtual teams, it's very important that you make the right choices about technological channels of communication which are suitable for everyone, no matter where, when or concerning what!

Track 21
Message 4

Voice: The person you are calling cannot take your call right now. Please leave a message after the tone.
Sam: Hi, Hans, Sam here. Could you give me a call? I texted you, but you never got back to me. It's about Guillem in Ghana. I don't really want to go into it on the phone. Call me when you can. Thanks.

Track 22
Message 7

Guillem: Hello? ... phoning you since midnight! It's four in the morning here. I had a call from Sam and she said some very unreasonable things about how I manage the market down here. Please call me.

Track 23
Message 8

Helena: Hi, honey. It's Helena. Jürgen's running a temperature. Nothing too terrible, though ... When exactly are you back? Give me a ring when you can.

UNIT 5

Track 24

Ana-Kristina: Virginia, I've been trying to think of how I can make my writing more efficient. At the moment, it takes me far too long to write what I want to say, because I don't really know how to structure my writing in a clear and concise way.
Virginia: What you need is a step-by-step process.
Ana-Kristina: What do you mean exactly?
Yashi: I think what Virginia is talking about is a process which gets you to identify the purpose of your writing, collect the relevant information you need to include, then think carefully about the reader, and above all, structure your language clearly and logically.
Virginia: Yes, that's right. First of all, you need to establish why you're writing, then make sure you have all the facts at hand. It's no use referring to a document if you don't actually have it close by to send as an attachment if necessary. Next, you have to decide what your reader already knows about the subject, what they need to know and how they like to receive information.
Yashi: Yes, in my experience, some people like a direct approach, with just the essential facts, while others prefer a softer, more indirect style.
Ana-Kristina: You mentioned structure, too. Um, what tips do you have about structuring my writing?
Virginia: Well, the key is not to use too many long, complicated words or too much technical jargon. Keep your writing short and simple. Try to have a mix of long and short sentences to help the ideas flow and to avoid misunderstanding.
Ana-Kristina: Your process seems a very good idea. I'll keep it in mind next time I have to write something.

Track 25

Alisha: Hi, everyone! Thanks for coming. As you know, we've done a lot of hard work on this latest innovation project, and the lack of positive response from senior management is extremely worrying. Obviously, we're doing something wrong and we need to take drastic action. Mika suggested that we invite along Robert—
Robert: Hi!
Alisha: —who's an expert in communication, to try and identify our weaknesses and help us to come up with a solution. So, welcome, Robert. Perhaps you'd like to begin?
Robert: OK. Um, let's start by thinking about what you're doing wrong. Can anyone think of anything obvious?
Alisha: Sanjeev, you have something to say on this?
Sanjeev: Well, I don't know if anyone else agrees, but it seems, when we meet the management face to face, everything goes really well. They like our presentations and are happy with our recommendations. The dialogue is usually very positive. However, as soon as we submit something in writing, their attitude seems to change.
Mika: Yes, I agree. When I send an e-mail, the response can be quite different. They seem far more reluctant to accept my suggestions and they question every little detail, as if they don't believe me.
Robert: So it's once you put your ideas in writing that things go wrong?
Sanjeev/Mika: Mmm./Yes.
Robert: It seems to me then that you could do with some training in effective writing. Right?
Sanjeev: Even though I was brought up speaking English, I find writing a real challenge. I was never a grade-A student at school, and nothing's changed! I write how I speak, and I suspect that's not good.
Robert: So, too wordy?
Alisha: Actually, I totally agree. I can never seem to say exactly what I mean in a precise way.
Mika: And I don't know how to, you know, link all my ideas together smoothly? It takes me ages.
Alisha: You've raised some interesting points, Robert, thanks. The next step is to approach HR to see if they can arrange a training course which focuses on writing simply, concisely and in a well-structured way.
Mika: With a special emphasis on those ... linking words.
Alisha: Great! Thanks again, Robert, for helping us to find a solution. Perhaps you can recommend a good training company?
Robert: Yeah, well, I do know ...

UNIT 6

Track 26

Interviewer: What impact can working relationships have on performance?

Ana Giménez: Well, at an individual level, I use a simple three-step model to show this. Firstly, the way we treat someone has an impact on the way people feel. Next, the way a person feels has an impact on the way they perform in their job. The way they perform will then have an effect on the way the manager, colleague, etc. treats them. So we have a self-sustaining circle, either positive or negative. Treatment, feelings and performance.

Track 27

Interviewer: Can you give us an example of how this model works in more detail?

Ana Giménez: Yes. Let's say you have a manager who treats a subordinate with arrogance and lack of sensitivity. That person may feel they are not valued, so they may well perform without the confidence needed for good outcomes, especially if they're unable to meet their manager and discuss this issue.
On the other hand, if they're treated with respect and encouragement, they'll feel good about their contribution and they're much more likely to perform well because they feel they belong, they feel committed!

Interviewer: So emotions play a significant role?

Ana Giménez: Yes, absolutely. We need to feel significant and valued. Many organisations simply do not think about the importance of relationships in virtual teams. For them, only results matter – even if colleagues never actually meet face to face.
It may not matter so much to a Northern European member if personal relationships are good or indifferent. They prefer to separate professional from personal. But when we have team members from cultures where personal and professional relationships cannot be separated, you risk creating a situation where at least some of the team feel less involved, and that can have an impact on performance.

Track 28

Interviewer: OK, Ana, so how can these positive relationships be developed in a virtual context, where teams can go for months or longer without meeting face to face?

Ana Giménez: That's a major challenge. If we think about how we establish relationships face to face, there are a lot of non-linguistic factors – eye contact, gestures or facial expression. These sensory clues can't be interpreted so easily, even on Skype or video. So we need to compensate for this lack of non-verbal communication.

Interviewer: How do we do that?

Ana Giménez: We ask more questions than we would normally ask. We have to spell things out much more. We 'manage' the communication more.

Interviewer: What do you mean by 'manage the communication'?

Ana Giménez: When we finish what we wanted to say, we need to explicitly hand over to the other person, so we could say 'What do you think?' or 'How do you feel about that, Juan?' … things like that. Ways of making it clear to the other person that now it's their turn to respond or contribute.

Interviewer: Oh, right, I see. So, Ana, what other factors are important?

Ana Giménez: One significant factor is the status of the people involved. If you have a manager at headquarters dealing with a team member on the other side of the world, the manager has to use sensitivity and cultural awareness to get commitment. This could be by communicating in a very different way to what feels natural, and saying what they *feel*, not just what they *think*. Silence is also a big factor in virtual communication!

Interviewer: Why?

Ana Giménez: Because it could mean so many different things. Lack of engagement, lack of understanding, anger, confusion or even not paying attention. In a virtual context, it's important to voice these issues and, if you are in a position of responsibility, it's important to use questions and other coaching techniques. That way, you have a real chance of getting a useful response.

Track 29

George: Our company's software platform includes the option of having a Facebook-style networking page. I set one up for my colleagues. We operate in Europe and Singapore, and at first, there was some resistance from some people to posting personal information on this kind of network. However, I spent time discussing it with the team and I made it clear that no one was obliged in any way to contribute to the page. That seemed to break the ice, because after a few weeks, most people were contributing – well, six out of ten colleagues. We haven't heard from the other four yet. I think it's fun to have pictures of your kids, family and activities to show colleagues on the other side of the world that you have a life outside the office! The social element is important – otherwise, we could end up simply treating each other as a kind of resourceful robot!

Track 30

Angela: When we set up the project group, I asked all members to produce a one-slide personal profile. I showed them an example – my personal profile – and presented it onscreen. It included information about my qualifications and experience and what I enjoy doing outside work. We had the meeting, and some were happy to reveal interesting and unusual hobbies – charity fundraising and paragliding, to name two – while others highlighted their family life and its importance.
A minority limited themselves to professional experience, qualifications and their professional areas of interest. I assume they liked the idea, because no one said they didn't.

Track 31

Viola: I tend not to set up a situation where everyone in the team thinks, 'Oh well, if it's Monday at four o'clock in the afternoon, my team leader will be calling for her weekly "chat"!' That, for me, is too formal, too predictable. I prefer to contact my team when I know that they're available, but without warning. I'm good at remembering a lot of information about their personal lives. For example, someone is pregnant, so how is she? Another is completing a Master's – how did the recent exam go? Another has just come back from two weeks' leave. How did the trip to Madagascar go? That sort of thing. And I share my preoccupations and stories with them. Why? Because remembering details like that shows I value them and that I'm interested and curious about what makes them tick.

Track 32

Michael: ... so I just feel the atmosphere in these conference calls isn't improving. We aren't moving forward. The team in the US seems to be forgetting that it was us who took them over, not the other way round! Huh, Marie?

Marie: Yes, it is that way, sometimes. Um, our working practices here in Germany are very good. I think you can convince them of that.

Michael: Not in the short term. And, as you know, I've been trying hard over the last few months. They just won't play ball! They *know*, but they won't admit it ...

Marie: Um ... Yes, I know. Michael, there's the San Francisco conference coming up soon. We have some time scheduled there. Can we organise a session ...

Michael: Yes! Yes, I think we need to prepare something. We need to decide quickly what we can do or say to change this, because if we don't, we'll have to wait another year, ...

UNIT 7

Track 33

Nils: Yes, I agree. You know, when we work for an international organisation, with operations spanning the globe, it's clear that it's very complicated to manage diversity. The culture of an office in São Paulo will be different to that of a German office or a subsidiary in Shanghai. In fact, different departments in the same organisation may have radically different ways of carrying out day-to-day activities. Heather, you've seen this diversity and its impact on your global teams, haven't you?

Heather: I certainly have, Nils. I've worked with many groups of people from different national and regional divisions, but there can also be diversity among staff of the same cultural background. I mean, I've found that many technical specialists will get angry at what they see as the impossible deadlines being asked of them by the urgent requirements of the marketing department. That can lead to conflict in conference calls and even written communication.

Nils: Yeah, yeah, I see your point. It's more complex dealing with diversity in a virtual context. We don't get so much opportunity for face-to-face contact, and we have less chance of spending 'downtime' together – you know, the chats we have round the coffee machine in normal offices!

Heather: And I also think there are more risks around misconceptions.

Nils: How do you mean?

Heather: Well, we can form an impression of someone which can be completely wrong in many cases. We decide we don't like their voice, the speed they speak at, their attitude. We can sometimes forget there is a human being at the end of the line, not just a resource!

Nils: Yeah, I've done that before now!

Heather: Anyway, Nils, you tell me ... what's your approach to dealing with this diversity?

Nils: Mmm, a difficult question. I suppose for me, it's critically important to plan how you're going to manage diversity before you start working with a group. That way, you can prevent some problems from emerging. I also think you should establish some kind of common procedure for dealing with them if they do emerge, although that's sometimes easier said than done.

Heather: Yeah, I'm totally with you on that!

Track 34

Nils: So, Heather, what are these key factors you were talking about earlier?

Heather: OK. Let's see ... Firstly, we need to allow for planning styles; some individuals will like detailed planning, others, a more organic approach, a kind of 'let's see what happens' planning approach. We need to work together, so everyone has to appreciate that there's more than one way to produce good results. Secondly, we need to get a clear set of rules for managing differences of opinion and conflict.

Nils: Rules?

Heather: Well, um, you know, guidelines ... some groups call it a 'team charter'.

Nils: So you think we can manage conflict if the correct structures are in place?

Heather: In an ideal world, yes ... But it isn't just a matter of structure. It's perception, too. For example, a person from a risk-averse culture may well be very resistant to the actions of a person who is risk-tolerant. This can mean serious disagreements in procedure. We need to bring this problem into the open but in a sensitive way!

Nils: OK, so we've identified the problem. And we have a process to manage it. What next?

Heather: We need to de-escalate the situation before it gets out of control.

Nils: That sounds worrying!

Heather: Well, sometimes, a problem can become personal quite quickly. I think we've all experienced that! You may say or write things you would see as unacceptable if someone did it to you. Escalation can mean going to a more senior manager. It can mean spreading the conflict. In the worst case, it could even mean people having to leave the group.

Nils: Phew, that's never happened in my experience!

Heather: It has to me. Very sad, it was …

Nils: Mm, I'm sure it was … Yeah, OK … Well, for me, another really important factor is different communication styles. From my experience, some people can be really direct, and if they deal with colleagues who are indirect in their approach, both find the other person very frustrating and even annoying.

Heather: I'm direct!

Nils: Yes, I know. Another thing is personality. I like personable and outgoing characters, but not everyone is like that. We need to adapt a bit – quiet and cautious people are equally valuable! We all need to be aware of why people are different, and how we can accept that and still work well together.

Track 35

Rajat: I prefer to speak to people one to one. I can get a better feeling for what the fundamentals of the issue are, I can ask more questions and I think it's better for persuading and influencing people in your favour! Conference calls? No way! A waste of time, just several people trying to speak at the same time, or a facilitator who acts like a policeman and doesn't let anyone finish.

Track 36

Henning: I'm not a very expansive speaker and I don't really like our international meetings by conference. I'm not a big contributor, er, and it seems to be dominated by those with the loudest voices and personalities rather than those who really know, you see? I'm happiest communicating in written form, because there is no ambiguous message – it's there in black and white. I can also express myself in a much more sophisticated way if I'm drafting an e-mail. Even instant messaging is a good way to have a conversation.

Track 37

Isabel: I really enjoy our conference calls because it gives me the chance to connect with other team members. It's good to hear their voices and, you know, to share and develop ideas with them over the hour the call lasts. Um, I'm not so enthusiastic about the amount of documentation – we need to store a lot of documents in the dashboard database – but of course, I recognise it is necessary.

Track 38

Rajat: I don't feel so happy with my writing. I can send instant messages and texts OK, but I really need to work on my longer written messages.

Track 39

Henning: Well … I suppose I'd like to contribute more in our weekly calls. I know I'm too quiet … I just find it hard to interrupt more confident or outgoing colleagues. Yeah, I want to be able to interrupt people and have my say.

Track 40

Isabel: I get bored very easily when I'm checking long documents for factual accuracy or correctness. Mm, I often do it too quickly. I should be more patient, yes … because results would sometimes be better!

UNIT 8

Track 41

Colleague: Martina, how can we lead people effectively when we can't see them?

Martina: Hm, well, I think that in order for people to work effectively virtually, there has to be trust – I mean, trust in clear goals and a strong interest in the team's well-being. I don't think trust happens magically, but it can be made stronger when you bring a team together regularly. The leader can then be more explicit about expectations, and can deal with the team's questions and opinions directly. So, if possible, try to bring your people together at least once a year. During that get-together time, a leader often gets a better idea about factors such as … such as an individual's working style, or even personality differences. These factors may not have been obvious when working purely virtually.

Colleague: What if we don't have the opportunity to meet them? Many global teams don't have that option, due to time, distance and cost.

Martina: Fair point! One way to get around not seeing people is for the leader to *model* the behaviour they expect of those they manage. That way, there's a, a good chance that team members will mirror, or copy, that behaviour. So, if you want your team to be punctual, collaborative and reliable, you need to actively demonstrate that *you* are punctual, collaborative and reliable. You can't promise action on something and then not deliver it. Otherwise, the team may just copy that behaviour – because it's the model which appears to be acceptable if the leader does it!

Colleague: In a physical office environment, 'being busy' can be seen as doing real and useful work. In the 'invisible' virtual world, we can't make that assumption because we can't see what the others are doing!

Martina: Yeah, absolutely! In the virtual environment, when you can't see what people are doing, actions don't speak louder than words. For a good virtual leader, the key is to be present, to be available. That means monitoring progress towards the results you want on a more frequent basis than if you were all in the same office. For me, monitoring acts as a kind of microscope.

Colleague: A microscope?

Martina: Well, yes. What I mean is that monitoring can reveal which team members need more hands-on guidance and which others can be left to act with relative autonomy. That doesn't mean that some people aren't working as hard as others! Just that they may need more support.

Track 42

Colleague: Martina, what about creating standards? Do you think having a clear quality standard helps to build high-performing virtual teams?

Martina: Oh yes, definitely. A leader needs to decide what his or her expectations are. So, they must ask themselves 'How do I define quality standards?' and 'What performance do I expect from my team?' ... I think making sure everyone knows the answers to those two questions is especially important when people are physically separated. In general, people need to have a very clear picture of the overall aim, as well as the way in which they are expected to operate. And they need to be reminded of that, um, 'big picture' more often than if they are physically together. Otherwise, the leader runs the risk of managing a group of people with different interests and priorities, rather than a team with a common purpose ... even if they never meet physically.

Colleague: People talk about virtual team cultures. What exactly does that mean, and how is culture affected by leadership?

Martina: Well, I suppose the definition is having a set of norms which every single person is aware of and that they willingly follow. Again, the challenges for the virtual leader are how to encourage, or impose, norms which benefit everyone, and that everyone agrees to.

Colleague: Can you give me an example?

Martina: Let's say a virtual team member is not responding to requests or queries from colleagues, and this is having a bad effect on the progress of a project. What happens? ... Do those colleagues simply wait? Do they inform the team leader and ask him or her to take action? ... A leader's style could be hands-off; they might say, '*You* need to work out how best to communicate with your colleague. My role is not to manage issues like this,' or the leader may say, 'If there are problems with availability or response time, I want to know about it and I will then get involved.' In each case, leadership style influences team culture one way or another.

Track 43

Dermott: So, everyone, I think we're all here, so let's make a start. Welcome to you all. Er, can you hear me clearly? ... OK.

This isn't a regular conference call, but I think it's really important to have it now, because if we can establish how we operate with a common understanding at the beginning of this project, it's going to make everything much easier, because we'll all know what we need to do. It'll be more pleasant, too, because we'll all appreciate each other more! It'll be more satisfying, because we can see the results of what we do. And, ultimately, I think we'll be more productive, which always impresses senior management, as you all know, no doubt.

There are a couple of tools I've used before on other projects and which have had a very positive impact on the team's performance in general. Um ... the first tool is the team clock, and it works like this. We start at midday and by the time each phase of the project is completed, we've reached midnight. Then we reset the clock for the next phase. OK so far? Yeah? Right, you can see the clock at any time on the team's virtual dashboard, and when you look at the time on it, you get an idea of where we are in terms of progress. Can you all see it on the screen now? ... Yes? ... There are two hands on the clock. The green one shows where we really are in terms of actual progress. The red hand shows us where we should be. If the two are at the same place, we're on schedule. If the green one is at four and the red one at five, we have a problem and we're behind schedule. If the green one is further on than the red one, we're ahead of schedule! As leader, I take responsibility for positioning the green hand, after my weekly individual consultation with each team member ... Er, right. Any questions so far?

Track 44

Dermott: ... take place later in the first phase. OK, I think everyone's clear about the preliminary resource allocation and task dependencies, yeah? So, before you all go, could I just briefly bring up another point?

Juanita: Em, will it take long, Dermott? I have another call at 12.

Dermott: No, Juanita, it won't. Look, it's just that we're working virtually, across four continents and in seven different places. That's complex in itself, for reasons of time difference, local demands and so on. I know you're all aware of this. You all have some kind of experience with virtual operation, which is why I chose you. But, based on good and bad experience, I think we need to consider having some kind of a team charter, to specify exactly what commitments we have to each other.

Roger: It's Roger here, Dermott. That sounds rather unusual. Er, what kind of charter, exactly?

Dermott: I mean in terms of behaviour – how we collaborate, how we manage knowledge-sharing. Right? So, immediately after this meeting, I'm going to send you a list of guidelines which I believe are essential for the smooth running and harmony of the project. I'd really appreciate it if you could each take a look and decide which rules, which guidelines are acceptable to you. How does that sound? OK?

Jan: Dermott, I'm not so sure what you mean.

Dermott: OK, Jan. Right, um, let me give you an example ... So, if the topic is 'Response time to e-mail received', you need to decide what the *maximum* reasonable and courteous response time is, er, 24 hours? 36? 12? That's the maximum, which doesn't mean that you can't reply earlier, of course.

Jan: Yeah, OK. Thanks.

Roger: Roger again, Dermott ... Um, this may be a stupid question, but why are we doing this?

Dermott: Well, all of us – and I include myself here – we all want this project to work smoothly and, in my experience, spending a bit of time establishing things at the start helps. I just want to be sure we have norms, we have a commonly accepted way of proceeding. Right. Any other questions about what

I've just said? ... OK, could you let me have your responses tomorrow by ten o'clock GMT? Thanks. Right, now, we have one more point to cover ...

Track 45

Jayne: OK. Has everyone managed to log in? ... Good. Did anybody *not* receive a copy of the agenda or the proposed sales initiative? ... Right, since time is short, I'd like to kick off by running through the initiative, which the management would like to introduce in the next three months, and then get some feedback from you all. As you know, Alain Dufresne, Head of European Sales, and his team have come up with this initiative designed to stimulate growth. Serina, what do you think of this proposal?

Serina: Well, I'm not happy. It's difficult enough trying to secure deals with existing customers in this current climate, so finding new customers is almost impossible.

Steve: Well, I don't know about anyone else, but I've got a lot of work to do! Hey, Clare, if you're making coffee, I'll have one – milk, two sugars. Thanks!

Jayne: Er, well, Guy, perhaps you can tell us about the current situation in Paris and how you think the initiative will impact on French sales?

Guy: Yes, thank you, Jayne. Actually, in France we're also struggling to win new contracts – um, the situation is as bad as everywhere else. Customers are looking for suppliers who offer the lowest prices, you know. We have to negotiate really hard to get any deals, and my sales team are very unhappy about this.

Serina: Tell us something new! We're *all* in the same situation!

Guy: Serina, please! I haven't finished!

Steve: Yeah, Serina, let Guy finish! You had your chance earlier.

Jayne: Er ... could I just come in here? Guy, can you summarise briefly? Then maybe Serina can speak on behalf of her colleague Tomás, who couldn't make it today?

Guy: As I was saying, my reps are not happy, and this is having an effect on my whole team's morale, and their performance. Sales are down 15% on last year! Fifteen!

Jayne: Serina?

Serina: Yes, thanks, Jayne. Tomás and I have been speaking together a lot about this economic crisis and, well, according to Tomás, Portugal is also suffering a great deal, too. In fact, neither of us knows what the solution is. Tomás couldn't give me any figures to back this up right now, because he's still waiting for key data to be analysed, so it's difficult to give you a clear picture. Sorry!

Jayne: OK. Right. We aren't getting anywhere with this. Let's finish now and have another call same time next Wednesday. Thanks for attending, and ...

Answer key

1 Understanding virtual communication

A 2 *Suggested answers*: e-mail, VoIP (Voice over Internet Protocol), phone, IM (instant messaging), texting, conference-calling, fax, social or business networking (e.g. Facebook, LinkedIn), photo-sharing sites

4

name	job	technology used	opinion/attitude
Bettina	project manager	e-mail, instant messaging, conference calls, Skype	• e-mail and instant messaging useful for solving problems • thinks written communication would save time • conference calls a waste of time
Ana	team leader	conference calls, phone, e-mail	• conference calls useful – achieve a lot • pleasant and committed team • friendly atmosphere
Chantou	factory manager	e-mail, phone, conference calls	• less positive – poor English • doesn't like conference calls • doesn't attend all conference calls as some content not relevant to her

6 a 1 g 2 b 3 f 4 e 5 a 6 c 7 d
b *Suggested answers*
1 phone, e-mail, Skype 2 conference call
3 phone, Skype, conference call, e-mail, IM
4 e-mail 5 conference call 6 IM, conference call, Skype 7 IM, conference call, phone, e-mail, Skype

7 a Sharing screens
b attend; weekly calls
c invest time
d files; send; attachments
e solving problems; real
f exchange ideas
g report to; senior managers

B 2 You may say that you communicate differently in different situations and are not always the same. This is a perfectly acceptable answer, but try to think of more general examples.
Suggested answer: In situations where there is conflict or there is a need to influence people, different styles may be used, e.g. less or more direct, depending on the desired outcome. People also change styles in their professional and personal lives. In order to reach a successful outcome, people may need to change their style to be more in line with their interlocutor.

3 He speaks louder than normal; he is clearer and more direct; he tries to think about how he can keep students' attention.

4 b T c F d T e T

5 a Knowing if students are following you; encouraging students to ask for clarification.
b Ask for confirmation at regular intervals; ask checking questions.

7 a a If I understand you correctly, you want to …
b What do you mean exactly by … ?
c You've made a valuable point.
d Yes, I see what you mean.
e Exactly!
f Could you say a little more about … ?
b *Suggested answers*
So, what you're saying is …
In other words, you mean …
I get what you're saying.
I go along with that completely.
Can you expand on that second point, please?
Can you enlarge on that figure?
I appreciate your point.
Well put!

C 1 *Suggested answers*
be flexible, be IT competent, be structured, be organised, be punctual, be able to work independently, be reliable, have interpersonal skills, be an active listener

2 a Blogger A: acting respectfully towards each other, thanking people for contributions, creating a sense of unity / team spirit / togetherness
Blogger C: encouraging people to be aware of different styles, managing group communication well and knowing how to use different communication channels for different reasons
b Agreeing to something, (emotional) commitment, engagement
c 1 Blogger B 2 Blogger C 3 Blogger D

3 a He created unity and improved performance by inspiring a sense of belonging.
b Because it makes sure that they perform to the best of their ability and that they have a loyalty to the team's objectives and mutual dependency.

5 b autonomy **c** predictability **d** reliability **e** trust
f self-awareness **g** team spirit **h** availability
i networking skills

6 b reliable **c** team spirit **d** trust **e** autonomy
f available **g** networking **h** predictable
i self-aware

D 1 b *Suggested answers*
Positive: simple, short, structured (Some of the others may be positive, depending on the circumstances.)
(Other positive qualities not mentioned in the box include adaptability, flexibility, language capacity, good listening skills.)

2 Erik: structured, turn-taking, brief, task-focused
Mercedes: unstructured, interrupting, expansive, people-focused
Haruka: unstructured, turn-taking, brief, people-focused
Monica: structured, interrupting, brief, task-focused

3 a T **b** F **c** T **d** F **e** T **f** T

4 *Suggested answers*
Erik isn't interested in talking about subjects outside work. Mercedes may be a little confused because Erik pauses when speaking or replying to her. Mercedes may think Erik doesn't sound very positive, whereas he is very positive. Erik and Mercedes may have different reasons for wanting to speak to each other, and this could affect their attitudes towards each other. The communication is largely positive, as by the end of the conversation, both are clear about what the purpose of the communication is. At the level of relationships, it is less successful, as it does not appear clear to either speaker what the other's style is.
Monica wants to attend to business in a fairly impersonal way, but Haruka wants to make some small talk initally. Haruka also sounds slightly worried because she didn't know Monica wanted to deal with detailed information, so when she realises she isn't prepared, it makes her nervous. As with Erik and Mercedes, it appears Monica and Haruka have different expectations from the phone call, and this could affect the impression they have of each other. The outcome of the communication is positive in terms of task, because they both understand what is required. In terms of relationship-building, it is less positive, as Monica does not take into account Haruka's more relationship-based communication style.

5 a a To find out news about a problem with a power cut in Bratislava and request an update very soon
b E-mail A is much more personalised than E-mail B. It also uses the 'pull' strategy for getting what you want (persuasion), rather than the 'push' strategy used in E-mail B (telling, not asking).
c E-mail A has lots of questions, a personal interest in non-work activities, an informal, friendly tone, and is courteous in salutations. E-mail B is very brief and impersonal, with no salutations. It has misspellings and typographical/lexical errors. It uses erratic capitalisation and is purely task-driven.

2 Preparing for successful communication

A 1 *Suggested answers*
Think about the type of people (their nationality) and how they prefer to communicate, the time difference, lack of visual signs, the importance of small talk in their culture.

3 a Preparation **b** Purpose **c** Process **d** People
4 a, c, d, e, f
6 b Decide on **c** Draw up **d** Circulate **e** Make **f** Confirm/Check **g** Go **h** Adopt **i** Achieve **j** Get
7 a decide on the timing
b adopt [a more] flexible approach
c circulated [the] (relevant) information
d achieved better results
e go through the process

B 1 *Suggested answer*: Those leading successful virtual meetings should be: organised, structured, a good time keeper, a flexible communicator (able to use a range of styles), inclusive, an active listener, able to engage and motivate others, a decision-maker.
2 The purpose is to give them tips for planning more efficient virtual meetings.
3 a Only invite those who really need to be there.
b By encouraging small talk
c Keep everyone focused equally.
4 a Think about the difference in time and plan to alternate the meeting times to suit everybody.
b Decide beforehand what rules you want to introduce and go through them at the start of the meeting.
c Test the technology before the meeting and be familiar with how it works. If necessary, ask people to dial in early to sort out any problems which may arise.
6 b take into account / (think about) **c** rules **d** dial in **e** sort out
7 a a 5, 11 **b** 1, 2 **c** 8, 9 **d** 3, 4 **e** 7, 12 **f** 6, 10
b direct: 3, 4, 6, 8, 11, 12
indirect: 5, 7, 9, 10
8 *Suggested answer*: Make sure the right people are invited, keep to the correct timing, send out necessary information beforehand.

C 1 *Suggested answer*: People feel the meeting is not interesting or relevant to them and so 'switch off' and do other things.
2 a When you need to reach an agreement or get people to contribute ideas
b Because there are no visual cues in virtual meetings.
c Because it will not necessarily generate input, as it is not directed at a specific person. Also, as an open question, it does not invite people to agree with the speaker.
d They feel more included and in control.
e It stops them losing interest or doing other activities at the same time.
f By describing what is going on in the host location to explain silences, thus making the meeting more 'real', and by reviewing and summarising the discussion as you go.

g Describing background events that are happening out of sight of the other participants, thus adding 'colour' to the meeting.
h Use a variety of different techniques, such as visuals or brainstormed lists, at different times.
i To make presentations with a high content easier to follow

4 a make b give c lead d present e hear f look at
5 a engaged in b involve c Motivate d reports e Call f consensus g Employ

D **1** *Suggested answers*
Attitude of colleagues to time: punctuality, response time for e-mails
How frequently colleagues have contact
How good the leader is: clear rules, contact with team members

3 c *Suggested answers*
Making contact with the right person: Managers must encourage knowledge transfer to ensure that expertise does not remain in the heads of certain people, but is understood by those working in other fields.
Getting the right information: People need the most up-to-date version of documents, as well as the relevant formats to process this information. This means clear and explicit requests for information where necessary, to avoid wasting time.
Getting information on time: People who work in departments which are extremely well organised and function according to strict guidelines will tend to prepare in more detail and focus on keeping to deadlines and strict time limits. Those whose culture is more relaxed in relation to time may feel it is unnecessary to be so controlled. They will therefore prepare less, work more organically and not necessarily observe time limits so strictly.
Understanding/Interpreting information received: Certain functional areas (IT, for example) tend to be very specific and detailed when interpreting information. Other functional areas may take mainly the gist (general message) from a piece of information.

3 Working in virtual groups

A **3** a Because all projects are interrelated.
 b He may be needed on the production line.
 c Sudden changes
 d She is not always sure everyone has understood.
4 a T b F c F d F e T
5 a bring [everybody] up to date
 b check
 c create [an] environment
 d encourage people
 e getting your message across
6 1 d 2 f 3 a 4 e 5 g 6 c 7 b
7 1 vii 2 iv 3 ii 4 i 5 iii 6 v 7 vi

B **3** 2 Imran 3 Susana 5 Jessica
4 **Subject of call**: Contamination in bottled water produced at the plant in last 24 hours. Batches of the product have already been distributed to outlets.
Objective of call: To take decision on immediate action
5 a T b F c T d T
6 *Suggested answers*
Positive aspects: All have the agenda, most participants use others' names for ease of identification, Richard manages the call reasonably well (he prevents interruptions, involves everyone and closes the meeting well, although he does not ask everyone to summarise their action points).
Negative aspects: Interruptions, names not always used (causing momentary confusion), slightly aggressive behaviour (Imran, at the beginning), François not as involved as the others (a question of hierarchy? Susana is his line manager).
7 a wanted to ask you
 b just to be clear
 c I'm absolutely certain
 d Can [I just] go [round and] check [you're all] happy
 e Have [you] had [the] chance to say
 f could [you and I] talk about [that] offline after
8 b clarifying procedure c starting / welcoming participants d moving to next item e finishing f dealing with technology g inviting opinions

C **2** a F b T c T d F e F
3 a 6 b 7 c 4 d 2 e 3
4 a 2 e 3 f 4 g 5 c 6 b 7 a 8 d
 b 2 suggestion 3 direction 4 direction
 5 suggestion 6 direction 7 direction
 8 direction

D **2** b *Suggested answers*
- **voice**: speaking at a moderate speed, articulating and enunciating clearly, building in repetition and redundancy
- **audience**: pre-presentation briefing, need for participation, Q&A, opportunities for interaction
- **preparation**: realistic quantity of content, support material, technology, design of visual material, delivery of information (all at once, or little by little)
- **structure**: aims, timing, clear 'roadmap'
- **technology**: using PowerPoint or other presentation software, using the cursor to indicate your place on the screen

4 Working with technology

A 2 M-business: 'M' means 'mobile'; in business-to-business activity, this refers to the trend towards using smartphones (such as the Samsung Galaxy or the iPhone) to carry out everyday business tasks, such as data transfer, messaging, and preparing and editing documents. For business to consumer, it allows for the option of purchasing goods or contacting retailers or suppliers 'on the move', without needing to be in front of a fixed computer terminal.

tablet-computing: This refers to the use of small, hand-held devices with relatively large computing power (such as the Galaxy tab or the iPad) for a wide range of tasks. A tablet typically has a screen size of 16–25cm, compared with a laptop's 37–40cm. Typically, it is also lightweight and, thus, highly portable.

voice recognition: This is software which allows you to give commands to a device to carry out tasks such as writing e-mails, leaving message reminders or dictating instructions for later use.

web-based apps: These are applications, typically of a small file size, which allow you to carry out very specific tasks. The fact that they are web-based means it is unnecessary to use a device with the software loaded onto the hard disk. The data is automatically saved on a remote server on the Web, so all that is required to use these applications is a reliable broadband (WiFi) connection.

the cloud: This is the virtual storage space on the Internet where you can keep files of all types, rather than having them stored on your hard disk. Some companies, such as Dropbox, Google Drive or iCloud, typically allow you 5GB of free storage. If you want to have a larger storage capacity (for video files and so on), you typically pay a yearly subscription fee. A significant factor around cloud storage is that of security – the hosting company has to ensure you trust them to keep your data safe from hackers and cyber criminals.

virtual dashboards: This is software for use by companies working virtually. Typically, it consists of a screen where you can access up-to-date files, check on the progress of a project, identify which people are working on which aspect of a project or even get a mini-biography of your colleagues. It is often seen as the key technological element of team organisation in terms of information gathered in one place.

collaborative suites: This refers to software (such as Cisco's Webex or Adobe Bridge) which offers a range of tools for group communication, e.g. conference-calling, screen- or application-sharing, instant messaging. All of these elements are typically integrated so that when you are using them, your screen offers you different communication channels, for real-time (instantaneous) use.

3 1 dashboards 2 recognition
5 1 stores data which can be easily accessed; allows direct communication between team members; some have emotional barometer
 2 greater mobility; better business results; hands-free messaging

6

speaker	advantages	disadvantages
1 Rohan		• Human error might mean files are not updated or stored correctly • Not the best way of checking team's emotional well-being
2 Birgitte	• Variety of tasks possible	• Multi-tasking will result in poor concentration • Too much information

8 a strongly believe b don't think; We feel c really not sure d really appeals to me e totally disagree with
9 b 5 c 4 d 1 e 3
B 2 a F b T c T d F e F
3 a S b S c S d A e S/A* f A g S h S i S j S
* Instant messaging can be both, as it depends if the two parties are responding in real time or not.
4 a results b tasks d synchronous e asynchronous g complex communication
5 He gives examples of both types of communication:
 • simple communication: a quick question, relaying specific or small amounts of information to a group or individual
 • complex communication: giving feedback to an individual team member on their performance, making a decision about a specific issue requiring input from several people at the same time
6 a complex b simple c simple d complex e complex f simple
7 1 f 2 g 3 b 4 e 5 h 6 d 7 c 8 a
8 a send [a] link; recording [of the] conference call b track [and] monitor; social-media traffic c install web-based applications d remotely access; secure user e back up; cloud-based f upload; sales figures; access
C 2 a 3 b 5 c 2 d 4 e 1 f 6
3 a Buying, installing or configuring hardware or software, or hiring people to get it working
 b A monthly or annual per-user subscription fee
 c Get a free trial to evaluate the suite
 d Working together in the same way with shared procedures, processes and tools
 e Digital information has grown very quickly, and devices are more varied nowadays.
 f They are highly integrated: *a unified solution that makes it easier to find, share, manage and use information, and to locate and connect with the people you need when you need them.*
5 a operating b application c volume d coverage e access f password g firewall h filter i spam j reserve k remote l log-on m incident ticket n tablet

D 2 *Suggested answers*
  a face-to-face, phone call
  b e-mail, phone call
  c phone call, instant messaging
  d conference call, e-mail
  e face-to-face, conference call, e-mail

5 Effective writing

A 2 a *Suggested answer*: Comments A and C could have been made by non-native speakers who are unfamiliar with forms of address in different cultures and the lack language to write concisely.
  3 a 1 Establish why you're writing
    2 Make sure you have all the relevant information
    3 Decide what your reader already knows, what they need to know and how they like to receive information
    4 Keep writing short and simple, avoid complicated words and technical jargon, use a mix of long and short sentences
  b Make sure you have all the information you need to refer to or send.
  c Different people prefer different approaches: some direct, some indirect.
  d Avoid using long, complicated words and technical jargon
  e By varying the sentence length
  4 a hand **b** indirect **c** jargon **d** simple **e** mix
  5 *Suggested answer*: clear purpose, think about the reader, logical structure
  6 a collect **b** recipient **c** content **d** language **e** edit
  7 a 3 **b** 5 **c** 6 **d** 4 **e** 1 **f** 2 **g** 3 **h** 2 **i** 4 **j** 5 **k** 1 **l** 6
  9 a less formal **b** formal **c** formal **d** less formal **e** less formal **f** formal

B 2 *Suggested answer*: not too long, simple language, not too much jargon, appropriate register
  3 a The face-to-face relationship is good, but when they communicate in writing, something goes wrong.
  b They need training in effective writing.
  c Linking words
  4 *Suggested answer*: the importance of culture
  5 2 a 3 c 4 b 5 a 6 b 7 c 8 c 9 d, e 10 b 11 e
  6 a The meeting was badly organised. In addition, no one seemed to know who was leading it.
  b We have now missed the deadline for phase 1. Consequently, the project is no longer on schedule, and we will have to work much faster.
  c Many of the participants are unable to attend the teleconference. I have therefore decided it is better to postpone it for a week.
  d There has still been no improvement in team communication, so Ben has arranged a team-building activity for next Monday.
  e I thought my instructions were very clear, yet people are still not using the template which was sent out last month.
  f I would prefer to discuss this point at a later date. However, this is not possible.
  g I'm writing to let you know that no decision has been made on the new staff restaurant yet, although we have had some very interesting suggestions from employees.
  7 *Suggested answers*
    a ... I'm going to redraft it this evening.
    b ... he promised to circulate a document to clarify the main issues.
    c ... she lacks certain key communication skills.
    d ... the cultural differences need to be taken into consideration.
    e ... up-to-date statistics regarding the new factory.
  8 a As a result of **b** Therefore **c** Next **d** however **e** firstly **f** In addition

C 3 a F **b** F **c** T
  4 a To explain that the wrong system is being used
  b People are not following the standard process that they have been asked to.
  c He is going to check all the work done and ask for feedback from head office.
  d Remove the right to use the system
  5 *Suggested answers*
    a There is too much specific technical information. Francesco should highlight the main problems and their solutions.
    b He could summarise with bullet points and give clear action points.
    c Too many abbreviations are confusing and make reading and understanding the content difficult.
    d Threatened, angry
    e A meeting face to face is always better in situations where conflict may arise.
  6 The main message is to make the problems clear to the reader, then for the reader to understand the actions which need to be taken to rectify the problem.
  The essential information is:
  • Staff are using the HR Dev system (GZ12).
  • This is the wrong system for configuring payroll.
  • It has an impact on other specified tasks.
  • Stricter monitoring will be applied to the problematic tasks.
  • If nothing changes, users will be penalised.
  It is arguable that the last part of the e-mail sounds like a threat and adds nothing positive to the message. In fact, coming as it does at the end of the e-mail, the reader may well focus on that aspect too much.
  7 b His team leader announced that overtime was no longer allowed.
  c We permitted them to use our photos for publicity.
  d They recommended several ways of reducing energy in their report.
  e Everyone commented on the new canteen.
  f I prefer to call/phone than to e-mail.
  g May I suggest (that) we look for alternative suppliers?

D 1 *Suggested answer*: E-mail A has less information / background detail. Its objective (the request for a meeting) comes quite quickly. The style of e-mail B is less direct. It appears to consider the reader's feelings more than e-mail A (*For your convenience ...*).

2 a E-mail A is shorter, to the point and has two clear paragraphs.
b Because they want to identify exactly what the reason for writing is. More detail means less ambiguity or misunderstanding later.
c E-mail A

6 Building relationships

A 3 a 1 treatment 2 feelings 3 performance
b a sensitivity **b** valued **c** motivation **d** respect **e** encouragement **f** perform **g** valuable **h** committed

4 She mentions task-focused business cultures (e.g. northern European), where relationships are not so important, and people-focused business cultures, where personal relationships are important.

5 a Eye contact, gestures, facial expression
b We need to hand over to the other person to make it clear it is their turn to talk.
c It can be a killer – it can be difficult to know what it means: lack of engagement, lack of understanding, anger, confusion, not paying attention.
d Questions create a better chance of getting a useful response (because you can target the information you want).

6 b attitude **c** respect **d** commitment **e** curiosity **f** attention **g** self-awareness

7 b attention **c** curiosity **d** commitment **e** self-awareness **f** respect **g** attitude

8 1 g 2 e 3 f 4 a 5 c 6 b 7 d

B 3 a He decided to set up a social networking ('Facebook-type') page for his team.
b Not at first. Even after he spoke to them, only six out of ten contributed to the page.
c Because she wanted to lead by example.
d No, they included different levels of personal information.
e So that they don't expect it, it isn't too predictable
f Information about her team members' personal circumstances

4 a T **b** T **c** F **d** T **e** F **f** F

6 a b wavelength **c** mind **d** nutshell **e** wrong **f** straight
b b in a nutshell **c** get straight to the point **d** on the same wavelength **e** speak your mind **f** get the wrong end of the stick

7 1 e 2 b 3 a 4 c 5 d 6 g 7 f

8 a 1 happy 2 unhappy 3 satisfied 4 joking 5 confused 6 worried
b 1 Oh my God! 2 for your information 3 thank you very much 4 as soon as possible 5 See you later?
c 1 laughing 2 joking/confused 3 angry

9 *Suggested answers*
Some (e.g. *OMG!*) are very informal and should not be used unless you know the other person very well; others will depend on how well you know the other person, and some (e.g. *asap, fyi*) are perfectly acceptable in informal business communication, especially internal e-mails.

C 2 a They both demonstrate the importance of the trust you need to develop towards people who can often determine your future.
b Because it does not mean the same in all cultures. In Europe, it is acceptable, but in parts of Asia, it can be interpreted as a threat or rudeness.
c Thought, engagement, time investment, consultation and contributions from others.
d An environment where people can be heard and understood, where predictability, availability and mutual responsiveness and responsibility are the norm.

3 a observable **b** interpreted **c** informed **d** encourage **e** mutual responsiveness

5 2 i 3 f 4 j 5 h 6 d 7 c 8 b 9 e 10 a

6 a a 5 **b** 7 **c** 1 **d** 2 **e** 10
b a **To get on like a house on fire**: to have an extremely warm, positive and harmonious relationship with someone (a colleague, a friend)
To talk about everything under the sun: to discuss or chat about a wide variety of subjects, professional and social
b **What you see is what you get**: used to refer to a person whose character and personality is totally transparent, with no hidden elements
To be as regular as clockwork: (referring to work) to be punctual and reliable
c **To know something like the back of your hand**: to know a specific area of knowledge extremely well
d **To lay your cards on the table**: to be totally transparent in your intentions
To be economical with the truth: to withold information which may have negative consequences for the speaker; not telling the whole truth
e **To have an open-door policy**: to encourage or welcome personal contact in order to discuss or solve problems (often used to refer to managers in relation to their staff)
To get something off your chest: to talk about a problem that has been bothering you for a while

D 2 a Collectivists prefer harmony and getting along. Individualists are prepared to deal with conflict, even if they don't necessarily feel good about it.
b Some cultures believe emotions should not be expressed openly. These cultures would tend to avoid or minimise conflict as far as possible. Other cultures are encouraged to show emotions. They would face conflict head-on and be willing to participate, to reach a clear resolution.
c A raised (loud) voice in a conflict situation may be interpreted as arrogant by the other person.

Case study

2 *Suggested answers*
a The diverse levels of interest, involvement and commitment from the group members; Eric's clear reluctance to participate; no formal decision-making or leadership procedures; Michael's frustration
b Michael could raise the issue informally with Bob, outside the group; he could formally raise the issue as an agenda point for a conference call and request a more formal structure for the way the group is operating; he could avoid problems by simply not attending the calls (like his Singaporean colleague); he could wait until the face-to-face sessions in San Francisco and raise the issue with group members there, hoping to resolve the problem.

3 *Suggested answers*: team-building (business-focused and other); group brainstorming of procedures and action points acceptable to all; relationship-building opportunities outside formal workshop sessions

7 Managing diversity

A **4** a São Paulo, Germany, Shanghai
b Not liking someone's voice, the speed they speak at, or their attitude (forgetting there is a human being at the end of the line)
c Planning before the group gets together, to prevent possible conflict (as far as possible)

5 a a styles b detailed c organic d conflict
 e problem f De-escalate g out of control
 h direct i quiet/cautious
b Different communication styles and personalities

7 Planning: risk-tolerant, risk-averse, organic and adaptable, structured and rigid
Teamwork: individualist, flexible roles, defined roles, collectivist
Communication: argument-oriented, implicit and indirect, explicit and direct, consensus-oriented
Personality: personable and talkative, cautious and quiet, dependent, autonomous

8 a organic [and] adaptable; structured [and] rigid
b cautious [and] quiet; personable [and] talkative
c explicit [and] direct; implicit [and] indirect
d individualist; collectivist

B **3** See audio script on page 103.
4 a … improve his longer written messages (e-mails).
b … interrupting (colleagues in conference calls).
c … checking her documents for accuracy/correctness.

6 1 c 2 d 3 f 4 b 5 a 6 e
7 a 6 b 5 c 1 d 5 e 3 f 2 g 6 h 2 i 1 j 3
8 *Suggested answers*
a Thank you (very much) (indeed). / Good, (I'm glad).
b Sure, I'll get onto it right away. / OK, I'll send it (right) now.
c That sounds like a good idea (to me). / OK. Fine.
d Not at all. / OK, (I'll give her a call). / Sure.
e No, I won't. / OK, (I'll make a note of it).
f It's a pleasure. / Don't mention it. / No problem. / Glad I could help.
g Thanks.
h I'm happy it was useful. / Any time! / It's a pleasure.
i (That's a) good/great idea.
j OK. Don't worry, I will.

C **3** a The various ways of looking at the world, interpreting experience, solving problems and predicting future possibilities work together to produce a distinctive mental tool set, with a larger number of different strategies for problem-solving.
b Differing cultural perspectives, language and experience can also mean different ways of thinking about and defining problems.
c It is important to include the full range of interest groups most likely to be affected by a decision (and most likely to oppose it if they are excluded).

4 1 e 2 a 3 d 4 b 5 c
5 a underlying attitudes b disruptive element
 c cultural perspectives d nature; communication
 e conflicting priorities

6 *Suggested answers*
a That's not a very good suggestion. / That's a rather impractical suggestion.
b Could the conference call be in the afternoon?
c (I'm afraid) that might not be acceptable.
d Could I do it later? / I don't have time to do it now. / I'm afraid I wouldn't be able to do it now.
e That report he wrote wasn't (really) (very) good.

D **1** a São Paulo: 06:00, Sydney: 20:00, Tokyo: 18:00
2 a Some people may feel negative about always having to take calls at inconvenient times, when the caller always controls the time for meetings or phone calls.
b Give them more time to formulate longer responses or to clarify their understanding of other interventions. This may increase the chances of their intervention being more valuable than if you do not take these factors into account.
c Because some participants may feel less confident formulating verbal responses than others. If they have the time and opportunity to use the instant-messaging facility common in most conference-calling suites, their response is more considered and articulate.
d The time of day can affect our own physical well-being (metabolism, energy levels, sleep patterns). If it is not an optimal time, our performance or contribution will not be at its best.

8 Teams and leadership

A 3 a Trust
  b A leader can observe differences in working style and personality.
  c Being punctual, being collaborative, being reliable
  d To see which team members need more guidance and support, and which can act alone.
 4 a How do I define quality standards?
      What performance do I expect from my team?
  b The leader runs the risk of managing a group of people with different interests and priorities, rather than a team.
  c 1 'hands-off' (not interested in details)
      2 directly involved
 6 2 g 3 e 4 b 5 h 6 c 7 f 8 d
 7 b mediate **c** train/develop **d** provide/offer **e** store
     f inspire/create **g** maximise
 8 b *Suggested answers*
     Fairness in dealing with different team members' constraints
     Capacity to persuade and convince in writing
     Directive/dominant style when managing conference calls
     Good relationship with team members' local line managers

B 1 1 d 2 c 3 a 4 b
 3 a Much **easier**, more **pleasant**, more **satisfying**, more **productive**
  b a Behind schedule **b** Ahead of schedule
     c On schedule
  c Once a week (after his (Dermott's) weekly individual consultation with each team member)
 4 a iii **b** ii, iii **c** ii
 6 b productive **c** draft **d** charter **e** involvement
     f allocated **g** minute-taker **h** template **i** format
     j cross-reference
 7 a observe/follow; norms
     b attitude; conflictive/obstructive/rude
     c native language **d** specific aims/goals
     e limit; time **f** establish; aims/goals
     g positive attitude

C 2 *Suggested answers*
  Virtual teams need to put more effort into rapport-building and establishing trust so that members of the team can work together effectively in a shorter period of time; so the percentage could be higher for virtual working.
  According to the graph, team members also need to remain engaged, which means the percentage in this question might be higher, to reflect the importance of this quality for a virtual teammate.
  Virtual teams should be aware of the importance of sharing information with each other and make every effort to do so quickly and simply.
  Transparency and explicitness are essential, so again, this percentage might be higher than with teams who meet face to face frequently.
 3 1 c 2 d 3 b 4 e 5 f 6 a
 4 a Humour does not always translate into other cultures and can exclude those who don't get the joke.
  b At the kick-off meeting
  c The team should work together to establish them.
  d Culture or organisational or functional differences
  e Seek extra help from other team members
  f Yes
 5 *Suggested answer*
  The team leader could ask individuals to present themselves and their attributes, or a SWOT analysis could be done to highlight these points.
  The easiest ones to develop are practical ones such as 'learn the rules', 'go to school'. The hardest are 'be self-aware' and 'manage your expectations'.
 6 1 c 2 f 3 h 4 a 5 e 6 d 7 b 8 g
 7 a adapt **b** collaborate **c** own **d** responds
     e observe **f** Are; willing **g** knows/knew
     h am; responsible

D 3 *Suggested answers*
  It should be observed that it is very difficult and often misleading to identify an entire country as having a homogenous culture profile. In many cases, there can be significant regional differences.
  A Spain, Italy, Greece
  B France
  C the USA, the UK, Germany
  D China, Japan, India (Indian subcontinent: Bangladesh, Sri Lanka, Pakistan)

Word list

access (documents, files)	38
accessibility	63
account for	15
adapt to	42
alienated	15
appreciate	71
approach	18
asynchronous	40
attend (conference calls)	9
autonomy	13
awareness	59
back up (data)	41
background (detail)	54
benefits	78
best practice	30
blog	12
blogging	11
breakdown (in communication)	25
brief (summary)	33
browser	42
build relationships	9
business apps	39
buy-in	12
challenges	84
chat (room)	12
chat informally	14
check (understanding)	10
checklist	18
circulate (agenda)	29
clarification	18
clarify procedure	31
cloud-based	41
cognitive diversity	72
collaborate with	24
collaborative suite	38
collect (information)	48
collectivist	64
colloquial (language)	75
comment (*n*)	65
commitment	59
communication channel	18

compatibility	63
competing demands	78
complain	49
concise	10
conflicting interests	45
conflicting priorities	73
confused	35
consensus-oriented	69
control panel	43
copy in (cc)	19
core skills	82
correspondence	48
cost-effective	39
cover (an agenda)	29
create conflict	65
cross-functional	24
cultural factors	8
data storage	42
data-driven (presentation)	35
deadline	15
delegate (responsibility)	75
develop (skills sets)	79
discussion forum	12
discussion thread	13
disruptive element	73
dominant	79
downtime	77
draft (a document)	54
drop (someone) a line	60
effective (solution)	72
e-learning	41
encourage	35
encrypted data	9
engage	13
engagement	13
enquiry	71
equipment	29
expansive	10
explicit	69
expressive	64

fairness	72	keep (a meeting) on track	29	
fall behind	15	keep (a team) on track	75	
filter (e-mails)	51	keep people on board	10	
flexible	18	key factor	78	
four Ps	18			
framework	53	leadership	75	
friendship	58	lifecycle (team, project)	80	
functional speciality	78	line manager	12	
functionalities	41	log in/on	42	
gather together	29	manage communication	59	
gender	68	maximise (synergies)	79	
geographical distance	78	messaging apps	9	
get (a message) across	48	minutes (of a meeting)	15	
get feedback	31	misinterpret	61	
get to the point	60	miss a deadline	12	
get together	65	mobile device	40	
give feedback	53	module	41	
goodwill	13	monitor (a situation)	52	
group dynamics	68	monotone	64	
guidance	13	mood	84	
guidelines	49	mute (button)	32	
'hand-holding' culture	45	native speakers	60	
helpfulness	58	negative attitude	61	
humour	34	non-linguistic (factors)	59	
		non-native speakers	60	
identity	72	norm	80	
impact (on)	58			
implicit	69	objective	32	
impolite	48	operating system	43	
incident ticket	43	outcome(s)	19	
inclusion	63	overcome (differences)	25	
individualist	64	overload	42	
information flow	42			
inspire (trust, loyalty)	79	performance	74	
install	41	personable	69	
instant messaging (IM)	8	personality	68	
instructions	25	plain English	52	
integrity	63	plan (content)	49	
intrusive	12	positive attitude	61	
invest time	9	praise	33	
items (on an agenda)	19	presentation style	34	
		procedure	77	
job function	68	protocol	81	
judgement	13	purpose	52	
		put someone at ease	20	

range	41	turn up (volume)	33
rapport	20	turn-taking	14
react	63	Twitter	8
recipient	53	type (comments, e-mail)	32
reliability	12		
reminder	71	unified (strategy)	71
remote access	41	up and running	25
request	49	upload (files)	41
response time	38		
responsiveness	82	values	58
rich communication channel	44	variety	68
risk-tolerant	69	version	42
roles	18	virtual dashboard	38
		virtual teamwork	12
self-awareness	59	visual aids	18
send data	40	voice recognition (software)	38
sense of humour	58		
share desktops	40	way of working	24
share knowledge	39	web platform	15
skim-read	51	welcome (v)	31
Skype (v, n)	8	well-informed	59
smiley	51	willingness	82
social media	15	workload	9
social networking	60	writing process	48
spell check (n)	51	writing skills	53
stakeholders	9	written style	14
standard	25		
status	48		
stream (audio, video)	41		
stressful	30		
style guide	51		
supervision	80		
synchronous	40		
tablet (device)	43		
take turns	14		
team cohesion	74		
team spirit	11		
teleconference	11		
template	54		
thank	49		
time difference	54		
time zone	18		
time-conscious	35		
track (information)	42		
transfer (knowledge)	25		
transparent	51		

Notes

Notes

Notes

International Management English

International Management English consists of four titles covering key aspects of international business operations: *Leading People*, *Managing Projects*, *Managing Change* and *Working Virtually*. These four titles provide insights into the challenges of working internationally and develop practical skills which will help people to do their jobs more effectively.

Each book in the series consists of eight units, with every unit offering four distinct sections:

- *Discussion and listening* Engaging and relevant content in areas of international management and teamwork.
- *Communication skills* In addition to the familiar topics of meetings, presentations and negotiations, input and practice are also provided in conflict management, team building and giving and receiving feedback.
- *Professional skills* Authentic texts from management writers and thinkers provide the starting point for reflection and discussion among learners.
- *Intercultural competence* A focus on raising cultural awareness followed by an illustrative case study.

Leading People
by Steve Flinders

This helps new and experienced managers to develop leadership skills for working and communicating internationally.

ISBN 978-1-905085-67-5

Managing Projects
by Bob Dignen

This provides practical ideas on how to work and communicate effectively when taking part in or leading international projects.

ISBN 978-1-905085-66-8

Managing Change
by Fiona Mee

This focuses on the communication requirements of those either taking part in or leading business change, including how to handle resistance.

ISBN 978-1-905085-68-2

Working Virtually
by Jackie Black and Jon Dyson

This addresses the communication challenges that global teams face when using information technology to collaborate.

ISBN 978-1-905085-69-9

For full details of this series, please visit the Delta Publishing website:
www.deltapublishing.co.uk